Great Herb MIXES YOU CAN MAKE

Great Herb MIXES YOU CAN MAKE

Published by Long Creek Herbs
P.O. Box 127
Blue Eye, MO 65611
417-779-5450
www.Longcreekherbs.com

ISBN 1-889791-13-X

Contents

Introduction

I began my herb business in the 1980s. The very first products I developed were products that taught something, such as how to make a salve, or the steps for making an herbal hair rinse. The products included complete directions and a recipe, along with the herbs for making that product. Customers loved the products because they learned something while also making the product themselves. We sold these "Make Your Own" products in zipper plastic bags with a header tag. That method is efficient, inexpensive and shows the product well.

You can make these products yourself, for gifts or for starting your own business. In the Resources section you will find sources for buying good quality packaging and other items you may need. You will also find my business listed as a resource for bulk herbs. I have included examples of our packages, patterns, header tags and other items you may need.

Have fun making these products! Many of the ideas for them came from our own customers, through trial and error with lots of experimenting. I think you will find these formulas to be easy to make and use, and if you are making them for sale, profitable, as well.

If you plan to start your own herb business, these formulas and recipes are a good place to begin. Use them for your own products or adjust them to your own tastes and ideas.

As my grandmother always said, "Do what you most enjoy and everything else will take care of itself."

I love creating formulas and recipes, developing products and seeing customers pleased with what I do. I hope you will enjoy these recipes as you find those things you most love to do, as well.

Jim Long

Oregano
Chives
Sage
Herbs
in the
Kitchen
Bay
Dill
Basil
Tarragon

Beverages & Teas

We've sold the following teas for years in 3 x 5 inch zip bags with header tag, instructions and a tea strainer attached.

Herb Day Tea

We concocted this delicious tea blend for serving to guests as they arrived for our annual Herb Day in May celebration (we no longer have that event - it got too large to maintain).

1/4 pound raspberry leaves
1/4 pound hibiscus petals
6 ounces lemongrass
6 ounces chamomile flowers
1/4 pound rose hips
2 ounces spearmint
4 ounces lemon balm
4 ounces dried orange peel
2 ounces dried lemon peel

Mix well. To use, add 1 tablespoon mix to 2 cups boiling water. Remove from heat, cover and let steep for 5 minutes. Strain and serve.

Marvelous Mint Tea

2 tablespoons spearmint
4 cups boiling water

Cover mint with boiling water, cover container and let steep for 3 minutes. Serve with honey and lemon if desired. Serve hot or iced.

Cold Pressed Fresh Mint Tea

This tea doesn't work for a packaged product, but you'll love the flavor when serving it to guests. It's so fresh and aromatic that your guests will beg for your recipe!

Gather a large handful of fresh mint sprigs, leaves and stems both. Crush it up, wringing it a bit between your hands as if you were wringing out a washcloth. Put the crushed mint in the bottom of a pitcher, then fill the pitcher with ice. Pour water into the ice and let the pitcher stand for a few minutes before serving.

Southern Plantation Tea

(all ingredients dried)
1 cup raspberry leaves
1 cup lemongrass
1/2 cup hibiscus blossoms
1/2 cup chamomile flowers

Heat 2 cups of water to boiling then add 2 heaping tablespoons of the herbs to the water, stir and cover with a lid (it keeps the fragrant oils of the herbs from evaporating in the air). Cover and let steep 4-5 minutes, strain and serve. To serve as a cold drink instead of hot, add 1 cup of pineapple juice and 1/2 cup apricot juice to 2 cups of tea and serve over ice.

Raspberry-Herb Punch

We serve this to large groups simply because it's a beautiful beverage and because just about everyone of any age likes it. Even teenagers, who think they hate herb teas, like this! Use fresh herbs for this recipe if available, or dry if that's all you have. You can double the recipe and remove a quart of the liquid and freeze it overnight, to use in the punch bowl. Using regular ice waters down the punch too much when the ice melts.

1/2 gallon cranberry-raspberry juice
1 can (any size) frozen pineapple juice concentrate
4 cups water
3 or 4 entire leaves of lemon-grass, cut in 3 or 4 inch pieces
2 quart sized iced tea bags, Luzianne brand if available
2 cups dry hibiscus flowers or substitute several fresh red hibiscus or hollyhock flowers, green parts and center removed
3 lemons, sliced
3 oranges, sliced

Bring the 4 cups of water to a boil and add the lemongrass, hibiscus flowers, lemon and orange slices and simmer for 5 minutes. Add the tea bags, cover with a lid and let steep until cooled. Strain and save the liquid. Add that to the remaining ingredients, adjust sweetening by adding sugar to taste. Chill well (and freeze a bit for the ice of the punch).

When ready to serve, put the frozen punch in the punch-bowl or container and add the remaining ingredients. Float a few slices of fresh oranges and lemons in the bowl.

Hot Spiced Cider Mix

Assemble all of the dry ingredients and sell in zipper bag with recipe and directions attached.

2 or 3 pieces dried orange peel (or you can use fresh orange slice if making this for your own use).
4 three inch sticks cinnamon
4 teaspoon whole allspice
4 teaspoon whole cloves

Add the above ingredients to 1 gallon apple cider and 1 cup sugar and heat to just barely boiling. Stir to dissolve sugar. Cool and store overnight in refrigerator to let the flavors blend, then reheat and serve.

Bread Seasonings

Bread Herbs

These are delicious blends that work in bread machines or with hand made bread. An even easier method is to use 3/4 tablespoon of the blend to knead into thawed frozen bread dough. To make outstanding herbed dinner rolls, thaw the amount of frozen bread dough rolls, dip half of each roll in the herb blend and place the roll in a muffin pan, adding a second half, not dipped in the mixture. Let rise, covered and bake according to instructions on the bread dough package. These are so good! Use 3/4 heaping tablespoon, or more, of the mix per bread loaf.

Suggestion:

As a packaged product, place any of the following bread herb blends in a 3 x 5 inch zip bag. Print the directions for using the seasoning on the back of the header tag. Sell for $3.95 to $4.95 per package. These smell wonderful while baking and the bread turns out full of great garden flavors!

Garden Bread Mix

1 1/2 lb. parsley
1 1/3 lb. onion flakes
2 tablespoons garlic powder
1/2 lb. celery flakes
4 oz. oregano
2 oz. marjoram
1 oz. ground bay leaf

Mix and store in air-tight container. To use, add 3/4 tablespoon, or more, per bread loaf, kneading in before baking, or add to the bread machine before the rising begins.

Classic Bread Mix

1 cup parsley
1/2 cup onion flakes
1/2 cup celery flakes
2 teaspoons garlic powder or granules
2 teaspoons marjoram

Mix and store in air-tight container. To use, add 3/4 tablespoon per bread loaf, kneading in before baking, or add to the bread machine before the rising begins.

Sage Bread Mix

1/4 cup ground or rubbed sage
1 cup onion flakes
1 cup parsley flakes

Mix and store in air-tight container. To use, add 3/4 tablespoon per bread loaf, kneading in before baking, or add to the bread machine before the rising begins.

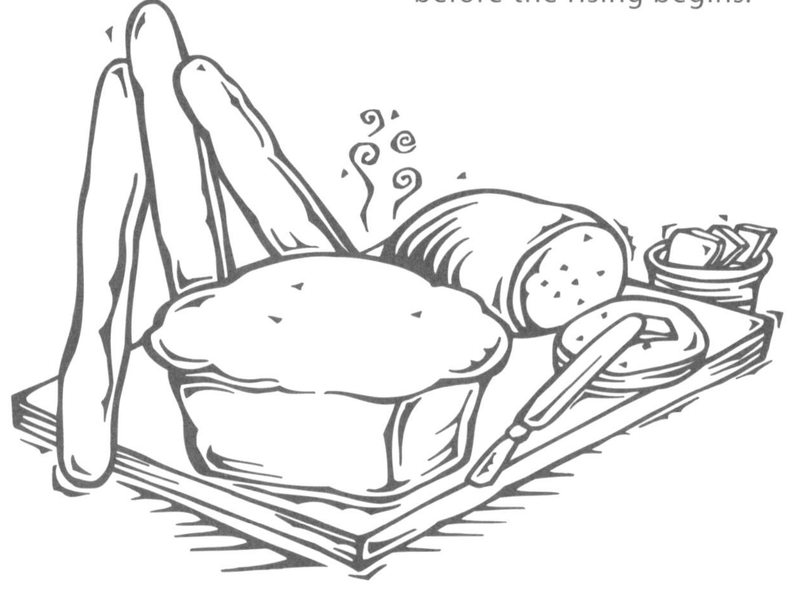

Herb Butters, dry

These make nice products to sell or give. We have always packaged ours in food grade plastic zip bags with header tags and instructions. All herbs listed are dry, but if you are making this for your own use and have the fresh herbs, use those instead. Increase the amounts of fresh herbs used as dried herbs are a bit more condensed and concentrated. The general rule is use twice as much fresh herb as dried, in volume.

The directions are the same for each butter blend:

Combine herbs and mix with 1 stick (1/2 cup) butter softened to room temperature. Mix well, mound into an attractive shape and chill. The butter should be chilled overnight, then brought back to room temperature before serving for best flavor. Butter tastes better than margarine in these recipes, so we recommend you don't substitute.

Note: Each recipe makes enough to fill one packet. We have sold these packets in a 2 x 2 inch zip bag, which is tucked inside a 3 x 5 inch zip bag. Alongside the 2 x 2 bag goes the recipe card with instructions for making the butter. The 3 x 5 bag is zipped closed and a header tag is folded and stapled in place. The product is then ready sales display or for placing in a gift basket.

Lemon Herb Butter

1/2 teaspoon lemon balm
1/4 teaspoon basil
1/4 teaspoon chervil
1/4 tsp chives
1 teaspoon parsley

Garden Herbs Butter Blend

1 teaspoon chives
1 teaspoon tarragon
1 teaspoon chervil
1 tablespoon parsley

Chive Butter Blend

1 teaspoon chopped dried chives
2 teaspoon parsley

Tarragon Butter Blend

1 teaspoon tarragon
2 teaspoon parsley
1/8 teaspoon onion powder

Dill Butter Blend

2 teaspoon dill weed
3 teaspoon parsley
1/8 teaspoon onion powder

Suggestion:

If making these to sell, use pound measurements instead of teaspoons in these recipes.
Remember that 3 teaspoons equals 1 tablespoon and 16 tablespoons equals 1 cup, when converting to larger amounts.

Herb Butters, fresh

While these won't work as a packaged product, they are delicious served to guests for special events. For example, if you sell a bread mix for bread machines, serving samples of it hot, with herb butter to your customers, will boost sales!

When I make fresh herb butter, I put all the herbs in the food processor and pulse-blend until well chopped, then I mix those with a stick, or more, of room temperature butter. After mixing, chilling the butter overnight gives the butter time to absorb the delightful herb flavors. Each of the following fresh herb butter recipes are to be combined with one stick (1/4 pound) of butter that is softened to room temperature.

Dill Butter, *fresh*

1 tablespoon chopped dill weed (that's the leaves)
2 tablespoons chopped parsley (flat leaf Italian, if available)
2 teaspoons chopped chives or green onion top
1 stick (1/2 cup) butter

Rosemary Butter, *fresh*

This is delicious to serve with roast beef or pork and even with beef stew. You can also use this mixed with butter to work under the skin of chicken or turkey before baking, for luscious flavor.

2 tablespoons fresh rosemary leaves, stripped from the stem, chopped in the food processor briefly.
1 teaspoon fresh lemon juice
2 tablespoons fresh parsley leaves
1 stick (1/2 cup) butter

Basil Butter, *fresh*

If you have one of the more red basils, such as Ruby Queen, Siam Queen, or cinnamon basil, use that for its surprising color. You'll like the butter on muffins, breads and homemade crackers.

2 tablespoons chopped basil
1 teaspoon fresh lemon juice
1 stick (1/2 cup) butter

Lemon Basil Butter, *fresh*

Lemon basil is my favorite of all the basils. Its pleasant lemony flavor compliments the underlying basil flavor. There are several lemon basil varieties, some with stronger lemon flavor than others. Keep the flower spikes cut off and the lemon basil will keep producing all summer long.

3 tablespoons freshly-chopped lemon basil
(loosely packed when measuring)
2 teaspoons fresh lemon juice, optional
1 stick (1/2 cup) butter

Marjoram or Oregano & Garlic Butter, *fresh*

Leaves from 3 or 4 sprigs of fresh oregano or marjoram, about 4-5 inches long, stems discarded,
1 clove fresh garlic
1 stick butter

In a food processor, combine the oregano or marjoram leaves, garlic and pulse blend until well chopped, then add 1 stick room temperature butter and pulse blend a few more times. Spread the butter on slices of French bread and toast before serving.

Cooking Formulas

Classic Seasonings

The following seasoning formulas are great for packaging in small shaker jars or zipper plastic bags with header tags. Customers love them because they are inexpensive and give delicious flavors. And, with these packaged and displayed in your store, the aroma of all of the fragrances makes customers want to buy and buy!

✯ Note: You can easily use pound instead of teaspoon in all of these formulas when making larger amounts.

All-Season #1

1 tablespoon each: basil, thyme and parsley
1/2 tablespoon each: ground bay and lemon peel

All-Season #2

3 tablespoons each (ground herbs):
basil, bay, thyme, parsley, lemon peel
1 1/2 tablespoon salt and black pepper

All Purpose Seasoning #1

2 tablespoon each (ground or finely chopped dry herbs):
marjoram, coriander, parsley & paprika
1/8 teaspoon dry mustard
1/8 teaspoon lemon powder
1/8 teaspoon garlic powder

All Purpose Seasoning #2

3 lbs parsley
2 lbs. onion flakes
4 oz. thyme
1 lb. rosemary
3/4 lb. celery leaf flakes
1/2 lb. marjoram
1/2 lb. basil leaves, cut and sifted
4 oz. broken bay leaves (or 1 1/2 tablespoons ground bay)
4 oz. sage leaves, rubbed
1 oz. garlic granules

Mix well and package. This is excellent seasoning for meats, stews, roasts and also vegetarian casseroles and soups.

Apple Pie Spice Blend #1

(Use 2 teaspoons per pie)
1 tablespoon cinnamon
1/8 teaspoon nutmeg

Apple Pie Spice Blend #2

(Use 2 teaspoons per pie)
2 tablespoon cinnamon
1 teaspoon ground fenugreek
1 teaspoon lemon peel powder
1/8 teaspoon each: cloves, nutmeg & ginger

Barbecue Seasoning

This is a dry seasoning to be rubbed heavily over beef, pork or chicken before grilling.

4 tablespoon paprika
2 tablespoon each: garlic & onion powder
2 teaspoon each: dry mustard & ground thyme
1 teaspoon black pepper
1/2 teaspoon cayenne

Barbecue Sauce

Add the above Barbecue Seasoning ingredients to:

4 cups tomato catsup
1/2 cup brown sugar
4 tablespoon prepared mustard
2 tablespoon Worcestershire sauce
2 teaspoon ground celery seed
1 teaspoon cumin
1/2 teaspoon ground coriander
1/4 teaspoon ground ginger

Mix well and brush on meat as it grills.

Bouquet Garni #1

Basically this is a small bouquet of herbs, 4 or 5 inches long, tied together with a cotton string. You can make bouquet garni and dry it, then package and sell it in cellophane bags with a header tag. Traditionally in bouquet garni will be parsley, sage, rosemary and thyme. I like to add a sprig of sage and one of basil, then wrap two or three leaves of garlic chives or regular chives tightly like a ribbon about the base of the bouquet.

To use: drop the entire little bouquet in a pot of soup or stew about half way through the cooking process. This adds a delightful flavor to broth, soup and stocks.

Bouquet Garni #2

Make the above bouquet garni, then surround it with two short (4-5 inches) pieces of celery stalk. Tie the celery around the bouquet with string and drop the bouquet into the soup pot.

Bouquet Cooking Wreath

These look nice in a clear cellophane bag with a header tag. This is a wreath made of herbs, about 5 inches across. Cut two 8-10 inch sprigs of rosemary, a few of basil, a green onion, garlic chives, sprigs of sage, thyme and parsley.

Use two of the rosemary sprigs as the form, bending them into a circle and twisting each

around the other. Weave in a sprig of each of the other herbs, wrapping the thyme and garlic chives around,and tucking in the ends. Within a minute or two you will have a tiny wreath. Wrap the chives or onion tops around like a ribbon. Put it aside to dry in an airy but dark place. In summer it will be dry in 4 or 5 days. Tie a ribbon on the wreath if you wish (but remind your customer to remove it before dropping the wreath in the cooking pot). Once you have made a few of these you will see how easy it is and you can make dozens in a short time.

Instructions for using the Bouquet Cooking Wreath:

Combine any meat and vegetables in a cook pot with water or broth. Bring to a boil, then slowly simmer. During the last half hour of cooking, drop the entire bouquet garni cooking wreath into the pot. You will love the flavor and aroma!

Bouquet Garni Seasoning

To add by the teaspoonful during cooking

3 tablespoon parsley
1 tablespoon marjoram
1 1/2 tablespoon basil
1 tablespoon thyme
1 tablespoon onion flakes

Grind or blend in a blender until the herbs are well chopped but not ground. Store in air-tight container out of light. To use: 1 tablespoon per recipe.

Bouquet Garni, *fresh*

3 sprigs parsley
1/2 bay leaf
2 sprigs thyme
1 shallot or leek (white part only if using leek)
2 whole cloves
2 celery ribs, about 6-8 inches long

Bind herbs and cloves between the two celery ribs, wrap and tie with string. Drop into cooking pot in last hour of cooking.

Bouquet, *fresh*

Many cookbooks of the past century call simply for the inclusion of a "bouquet." These were generally made like the following, using fresh herbs:

4 sprigs parsley
1 sprig celery leaves or young lovage leaves
1 bay leaf, fresh or dry
1 sprig thyme
2 whole cloves

Place the ingredients together, folding the leaves over like making a little package with the cloves inside. Fold over again and tie with string. Drop this bouquet package into the cook pot.

Bouquet Garni - *Long Creek Herbs version*

I like this fresher flavor, without the cloves of the recipe above..

3 sprigs parsley, Italian flat leaf if available
1 sprig rosemary
2 sprigs marjoram
4 or 5 leaves of garlic chives or standard chives
1 sprig any kind of basil

Tie all together and drop into the cooking pot. This is a delicious addition to soups and stews.

Bertha's Bouquet Garni

This version of bouquet garni was given to us by our friend, the late Bertha Reppert, of the famous Rosemary House in Mechanicsburg, PA, when she visited us some years ago.

12 tablespoons parsley, crushed
6 tablespoon thyme leaves
12 whole bay leaves, broken
1 teaspoon whole celery seed
24 whole cloves
36 peppercorns

Mix and store in air-tight container. Use 2-4 teaspoons tied in cheesecloth for average recipe. This looks nice in plastic zip bags or small decorative spice jars.

Bouquet Garni #3

1 cup marjoram
1 cup parsley
1/2 cup rosemary
1/2 cup thyme
3 bay leaves, broken

Mix and store. Use 1 tablespoon of mix for large pot of stew or soup (6 quart size).

Cajun Blackened Seasoning

2 teaspoon paprika
1 teaspoon each: black pepper basil, cumin seed, caraway, fennel, thyme, oregano and white pepper.
1/2 teaspoon each: crushed red pepper and salt

Grind or blend well to a fine powder. Sprinkle liberally over fish or chicken before grilling or cooking in a very hot skillet.

Chinese Five Spice Seasoning

(all ingredients ground)

1 tablespoon each cinnamon and star anise
1/2 teaspoon each: fennel seed, black pepper and cloves

Blend all well. Use with Asian dishes, poultry, pork and stir-fry. This is also the spice blend for Five Spice Chinese eggs, a delightful spicy, pickled egg delicacy.

Chili Powder #1

3 tablespoon paprika
2 tablespoon cumin
1 tablespoon each: turmeric, garlic, cayenne and salt.

Chili Powder #2

2 large dried pasilla chilies
1 large dried ancho chili
2 tablespoon dried oregano
1 tablespoon garlic salt.
2 teaspoon cumin seeds
1/2 teaspoon whole cloves
1/2 teaspoon coriander seeds
1/2 teaspoon whole allspice berries

Remove seeds and stems of peppers and tear the peppers into small pieces. Combine the chilies in a skillet with the cumin, cloves, coriander and allspice, stirring continuously over low heat for about two minutes. Pour out into bowl and let cool. Combine in small batches in food processor or blender, processing to a fine powder. Use about 1 tablespoon per batch of chili.

Chili - Quick Method

In a large cooking pan, heat 2 tablespoons cooking oil. Add 1 pound ground beef or ground chuck. Brown the beef in the hot oil. As it cooks, add 3 tablespoons of any of these chili powders, mix and continue browing the meat.

Add 1/2 onion, diced and cook until the onions are tender and transparent - about 8 minutes, stirring all the while.

Add 2 small cans of tomato sauce or one 8 oz. can of tomatoes and an equal amount of water.

Add your favorite beans - about a quart. We like half pinto beans and half pork and beans. Mix and simmer well until the liquid is reduced slightly. With a potato masher, mash up the chili, breaking up some of the beans. This thickens the chili.

Sometimes at this point I add some diced sweet pepper, a few sliced fresh mushrooms and possibly a hot pepper, then simmer a bit longer.

Chili - Vegetarian

In a large cooking pan, heat 6 tablespoons cooking oil. Add 4 cups raw, chopped soybeans (whir them up in the blender to chop them). Brown the soybeans in the hot oil. As it cooks, add 3 tablespoons of any of the above chili powders, mix well, add 1/2 onion, diced and continue cooking for about 5 minutes. Cook until the onions are tender and transparent.

Add 2 small cans of tomato sauce or one 8 oz. can of cooked, diced tomatoes and an equal amount of water.

Add your favorite beans - about a quart. We like half pinto and kidneys beans for this. Mix and simmer well until the liquid is reduced slightly. I add a hot pepper near the end of cooking. Serve this with sour cream, grated cheddar cheese and some chopped, fresh cilantro. We like it with cornbread on the side.

Court Bouillon

2 tablespoon onion flakes
2 tablespoon parsley
1 crushed bay leaf
1/2 teaspoon whole peppercorns
2 teaspoon each: thyme, fennel seed, celery leaves
6 sage leaves

Use 1 tablespoon tied in cloth for seasoning liquids, to poach fish, for seafood and poultry.

Curry

Curry powder is mostly a British invention to imitate Indian curry flavors. I've traveled on the Indian subcontinent, researching this seasoning blend and there is no such single thing as "curry powder." Still, there are several blends that give a pleasant curry-like flavor to foods. The seasoning, garam masala, is used for curry dishes and is made up in Indian households, the seeds being ground by hand in a mortar and pestle. Each family and each region has its own distinctive blend of these ingredients. The powdered seasoning is used with sautéed onion, garlic with other vegetables being added during the cooking process. Still, you can buy seasonings called "curry" in American grocery stores and make dishes that taste somewhat like those with the authentic Indian spice blends. Here are some that you may like, and that will sell well in your shop.

Curry Powder #1

2 tablespoon ground coriander
2 tablespoon fenugreek
1 1/2 tablespoon cayenne
1/2 teaspoon cumin
1/2 teaspoon white peppercorns
1/2 teaspoon ginger

Grind well and store. To use: sauté to nearly browned, a bit of garlic and onion, then add 1-2 teaspoon of the above mixture before adding the vegetables (potatoes, chickpeas, lentils, etc.).

Curry Powder #2

This one is a bland, very mild seasoning but for those wishing only a hint of the exotic flavor, it may be acceptable. Curries are generally a more complex mixture of flavors.

(All ingredients ground)
4 tablespoon coriander
3 tablespoon turmeric
2 tablespoon cumin

Curry Powder #3

6 tablespoon coriander
1 tablespoon each: turmeric, fenugreek and cumin
1/2 tablespoon green cardamom seed, peeled
1/2 teaspoon ground cloves
1/8 teaspoon cayenne

Grind well and store in air-tight container.

Curry Powder #4

3 tablespoon coriander seed
2 tablespoon ground turmeric
1 tablespoon cumin seed (or 3/4 tablespoon ground seed)
3/4 tablespoon ground mustard
2 1/2 teaspoon fenugreek
1 teaspoon green cardamon seed, peeled
1/8 teaspoon each: ground cloves and cinnamon
1/2 teaspoon each: ground mace and grated nutmeg

Grind everything well in blender or by hand in mortar and pestle. Store in air-tight container until ready to package. Curry powders, packaged in zip plastic bag with header tag, will make your shop smell wonderful and will entice customers to buy.

Curry Powder #5

1 oz. each: ginger, coriander and green cardamom, all ground to a fine powder.
1/4 oz. cayenne
3 oz. turmeric

Curry Powder #6

3 tablespoon coriander seeds
2 tablespoon ground turmeric
1 tablespoon mustard seeds
2 teaspoon toasted, dried hot peppers
1 teaspoon ground cardamom
1 1/2 teaspoon fenugreek
6 whole cloves
1 two-inch cinnamon stick, broken
1/2 teaspoon ground mace
1/2 teaspoon grated nutmeg
1 teaspoon cayenne pepper

Combine fenugreek, cardamom, coriander seed, cumin, mustard, cloves and cinnamon on a cookie sheet. Bake in slow oven (225°) for fifteen minutes. Cool. Add remaining ingredients and grind all in a spice mill or blender to a fine powder. Store in airtight container until ready for packaging.

Filé Powder or Gumbo Filé

Filé powder is used both for seasoning and to slightly thicken Cajun-style gumbos. The seasoning is generally a gourmet store item but easily made if you have access to sassafras trees.

To make the filé gumbo, gather young, tender sassafras leaves in early summer. Dry the leaves in a food dehydrator. Or, if you don't have a dehydrator and only want to dry a pound or so of leaves, place double handfuls in a brown paper bag, close it with a clothes pin and place the bag in the trunk of your car. Every day or so, shake the bag and place it back in the car trunk. The leaves should be dry and crispy in about a week. Remove the leaves from the bag and crumble them up into your blender and pulse blend until you have achieved a fine powder. Store it in an airtight container, out of light. To use, simply add about a tablespoonful of the Filé Gumbo powder to a soup, stew or gumbo during the last 15 minutes of cooking, stirring well as it cooks.

Fines Herbs

Fines herbs are a delicate blend of herbs, generally fresh, for sauces, soups, cheese and non-sweet egg dishes. When fresh fines herbs aren't available, or for packaging for sale, dry herbs such as these, are a good substitute.

Fines Herbs, *dry* #1

1 cup parsley
1 cup chervil
1/2 cup tarragon
1/2 cup chives

Fines Herbs, *dry* #2

1 tablespoon each:
tarragon, chives, chervil, parsley

Mix well, crushing or chopping in blender. Use with eggs, meat, fish and cheese dishes.

Fines Herbs, *dry* #3

1 tablespoon each: marjoram, parsley, sage, summer savory, thyme and celery leaf.
1 teaspoon black pepper.

Crush or blend well.

Fines Herbs, *fresh*

3 tablespoons parsley
2 tablespoons chives
1 tablespoon tarragon
1 tablespoon chervil

Chop herbs and use immediately. May be refrigerated over night or frozen in oil. Use in soup stock. For stocks that simmer for extended periods, add fines herbs in the last 10 minutes of cooking. Also use to sprinkle over soup just before serving.

Fish Seasoning Blend #1

1 tablespoon each:
tarragon, parsley, lemon thyme, summer savory
1/2 tablespoon chives
1 bay leaf crushed

Grind well. Use 1 tablespoon for each 2 pounds fish. Can be mixed in corn meal or cracker crumbs as a coating before grilling or broiling.

Fish Seasoning Blend #2

1 tablespoon each:
basil, tarragon, chervil, marjoram and parsley.

Fish Broil

Do you want good flavored fish that isn't fried? This is a simple blend that gives great flavor on broiled or baked fish.

2 cups celery leaf flakes
1 1/2 cups lemon basil (or substitute regular basil)
1 1/2 cups lemon or regular thyme
1/8 cup fennel seed (crack it in the blender if you choose)
6 cups parsley
3 cups lemon balm
1/2 cup marjoram
1/8 cup onion powder
2 tablespoons chervil

Mix well and store in an airtight container. To use, take out 1-2 tablespoons of the mixture and mix it with 1 cup cornmeal, cracker crumbs or bread crumbs. Mix. Roll fresh fish in the mixture, coating all sides and lay in a baking dish. Lightly spray the top of the coated fish with cooking spray, and bake or broil.
Crush or blend well.

Four Spices

(also called Spice Parisienne or Quatre Epices)

1 teaspoon each: cloves, nutmeg and ginger
1 tablespoon cinnamon

Mix well and store. To use: sprinkle on meats and sweet dishes. Good in apple pie, on bread or rice pudding.

Five Spice Powder #1

Equal amounts of each: star anise, fennel, pepper, cloves and cinnamon. Grind or blend to a fine powder and store in air-tight container. Use on roasted meats, poultry, oriental dishes. Sell by the ounce or in plastic zip bag with header.

Five Spice Powder #2

1 tablespoon freshly ground Szechwan peppercorns (1 heaping tablespoon before grinding)
1/2 teaspoon ground cloves
1 tablespoon ground cinnamon
1 tablespoon ground fennel seed
6 whole star anise, ground fine

This is a very old formula dating back to the ancient trade routes of Persia. The spices not only enhanced the food, usually meat, but also helped to preserve it. Fennel and cloves are still used as a digestive aid in India and surrounding countries.

Garlic Salt, *dry*

2 tablespoons garlic powder
1 cup salt

Mix well and store in a reliably airtight container.

Garlic Salt, *fresh*

Equal amounts of each: star anise, fennel, pepper, cloves and cinnamon. Grind or blend to a fine powder and store in airtight container. Use on roasted meats, poultry, oriental dishes. Sell by the ounce or in plastic zip bag with header.

Ginger Sugar

2 cups sugar
1/2 cup ground ginger

Use to flavor ham glaze, cakes, cookies, frostings. Sell this in a zip plastic bag or shaker jar, with a header tag and recipe attached.

Good Seasoning Blend

This is a tasty blend of herbs for soups, stews and chicken, pork and beef roasts. Use 1-2 tablespoons of Good Seasoning Blend for a pot of stew or roast, usually adding the seasoning in the last 30 minutes of cooking time.

2 cups onion flakes
3/4 cup celery flakes
1/2 cup marjoram
2 tablespoons sage leaves
1 teaspoon garlic granules
2 broken bay leaves
1/2 cup basil
2 teaspoons thyme
4 cups parsley
1 cup rosemary

Greek Seasoning

2 tablespoons each:
onion powder, paprika, black pepper, oregano and bell pepper.
1 tablespoon basil
2 teaspoon lemon thyme (or substitute 1/2 teaspoon dehydrated lemon juice or powdered lemon peel with 1 and 1/2 teaspoons dried thyme)

Grind to a fine powder. Use with lamb and pork dishes.

Gremolata, *fresh*

Seasoning for gravies and sauces

All ingredients fresh:
2 tablespoons finely chopped parsley
1 clove minced garlic
1/2 teaspoon grated lemon rind

Sprinkle this on sauces or gravy in the last 5-7 minutes of cooking. Cover pan for remainder of cooking to allow the flavors of the herbs to be absorbed into the liquid rather than going out of the cook pot in the steam.

Herbs de Provence #1

2 tablespoons each:
rosemary, thyme and oregano

Crush and mix. Use 1-2 tablespoons for average soup or poultry. For meat, poultry and stews.

Suggestion:

Sell Greek Seasoning or Herbs de Provence with an attached recipe card. The customer is more likely to buy the spice if they see the recipe and smell the ingredients!

Herbs de Provence #2

1 tablespoon each: thyme, rosemary and savory
2 teaspoons each: basil and tarragon

Crush well. Tie 1 tablespoon in cloth for average cooking pot then discard after cooking.

Holier-Than-Thou Salt

Use this seasoned salt on salads, casseroles, even on corn on the cob. If making this for sales in your shop, be sure to seal it up tight in a shaker jar or other container so that the salt doesn't draw moisture.

2 cups fine-to-medium granule sea salt, or Kosher salt
1 tablespoon black pepper
1/2 tablespoon parsley leaf, ground fine
1 teaspoon onion powder
1/2 teaspoon garlic powder
1 teaspoon celery leaf powder (or substitute celery salt)
1/4 teaspoon mild cayenne pepper

Italian Seasoning #1

1/2 cup each: parsley, basil, marjoram
1/4 cup each: thyme and rosemary

Grind in blender or food processor (or if you want to be authentic and you have a lot of time, grind it with a mortar and pestle).

Italian Seasoning #2

2 tablespoons oregano, marjoram, thyme, basil leaves, all crushed
1 tablespoon each rosemary and sage

Coarsely grind or blend. Use in spaghetti sauces and other oil or tomato based dishes.

Suggestion:

In case you forget: Any recipe calling for teaspoons or tablespoons, can easily be converted to cups or pounds. Simply insert the larger amount and you have a bigger mix! And 1 tablespoon equals 3 teaspoons.

Italian Seasoning #3

2 tablespoons each: oregano, thyme, basil
1 tablespoon each black pepper, bell pepper, chives
1 teaspoon tarragon

Grind to a coarse texture and store in airtight container or package for sales.

Italian Seasoning #4

Equal parts oregano, marjoram, thyme, basil.
Optional: half as much garlic powder and parsley.

Mix all blend to a coarse powder, or use crumbled.

Italian Seasoning #5

(for making Italian sauces)

1 tablespoon each: marjoram, basil and thyme
3/4 teaspoon peppercorns
10 cloves
2 teaspoon salt
1/8 teaspoon cinnamon

Mix ingredients, leaving whole. To make tomato sauce combine: 1 clove minced garlic, 6 quarts fresh peeled tomatoes (Roma or other paste type variety), 3/4 cup chopped onion, one stalk diced celery. Combine and simmer slowly for several hours. Add half of the above seasoning in the last hour of cooking. Taste and add more if desired. Serve over pasta, spaghetti squash or other vegetables.

Italian Seasoning, *fresh*

All fresh herbs:
4 tablespoons oregano leaves
3 tablespoons marjoram leaves
2 tablespoons (or 2 six-inch sprigs) rosemary
3 sprigs thyme
4 cloves garlic, crushed
1 whole onion, diced
1/4 cup chopped celery

Add this to 8 cups tomato sauce and simmer slowly for several hours. Adjust with salt and pinch of sugar if desired.

Marinade

2 tablespoons parsley
2 teaspoon garlic flakes
1 teaspoon each: tarragon and thyme
1/8 teaspoon ground bay

Mix with 1 cup red wine and 1/2 cup light oil (like sunflower or canola). Pour over chicken, beef or pork in a zipper gallon sized plastic bag. Refrigerate for several hours, or overnight, turning the bag occasionally to re-coat the meat. Drain off marinade and bake or grill.

Marinade, *fresh*

2 cloves fresh garlic, minced
1 bay leaf, crushed or broken
1 small onion, diced
2 teaspoons fresh thyme leaves, stem removed
1/2 cup Italian flat parsley leaves, chopped
1 teaspoon tarragon leaves
2 cups red wine
1/2 cup light cooking oil

Mix well and pour over chicken, beef or pork. Cover or place in zipper plastic bag and refrigerate for several hours or overnight. Drain and bake or grill.

Mexican Seasoning

2 tablespoons chili pepper
1 tablespoon each:
garlic powder, onion powder, paprika, oregano
2 teaspoons each:
cumin, ground celery seed and cayenne
1 teaspoon ground bay leaf

For meat, bean or vegetable dishes. Use 1-2 teaspoons per average dish, or to taste.

Mustards

Mustards are easy to make and have a fresher flavor than the bottled, commercial kind. We packaged the ingredients in 3 x 5 zip bags, with the recipe and list of ingredients, and all of that packaged inside in a 4 x 6 inch zip bag with header tag. This is a good item for including in gift baskets and for those who want to find items to make their own gifts for the holidays.

If you choose to make already prepared mustards in jars to sell, you should first check with the state regulations regarding food preparation in your state. Your local State Extension service or state university can direct you to an address or contact for that.

Mustard, Homemade

1/2 cup sugar
1/2 cup cider vinegar
1 oz. dry mustard
pinch salt.
Mix well, cover and let stand overnight in refrigerator.
The following day, add 2 beaten eggs

Cook slowly until thickened. Store in jars in refrigerator.

Mustard, Basic Sweet

1/2 cup sugar
1/2 cup cider vinegar
1 ounce dry mustard
pinch salt

Mix well, cover and let set overnight in refrigerator. The following day, add 2 beaten eggs. Cook slowly until thickened. Store in small jars in the refrigerator.

Mustard, Chinese Hot

(To sell as a dry mix that the customer makes at home, with a recipe card attached, or as a prepared mustard to sell in jars).

To sell as a prepackaged "kit" (with header tag and instructions): 1/4 cup ground oriental mustard seed in zip bag.
Place the instructions in a 4 x 6 inch zip bag, adding the smaller 3 x 5 inch zip bag of ground mustard inside. Attach a header tag and the product is ready for sale.

Combine:
1/4 cup boiling water
1/4 cup mustard powder
Mix well.
Add 1 teaspoon cooking oil and mix again.

Store in refrigerator; will keep for several weeks.
Use on egg rolls, sandwiches and other foods.

Mustard, Asian Hot

This is another version of the above Chinese Hot Mustard. It is deliciously hot for using on egg rolls. You can age this for a week or two but if you like it really hot, serve this mustard the day after you've made it, when it will be a its hottest. The longer it ages, the milder it gets.

1 cup dry mustard
3/4 cup filtered or mineral water

Mix mustard and water together and store in plastic or glass container in refrigerator until ready to serve. It will keep several weeks in the refrigerator.

Mustard, Old English Style

This is the authentic mustard served in English pubs with hamburgers, salami and sausages. Real pubs make this up every day but you can make up a batch and keep it in the refrigerator for a week or so. As with other mustards, this gets milder as it ages.

1/2 cup dry mustard
1/4 cup brown sugar
1/2 teaspoon salt
1/8 teaspoon tumeric
3 ounces dark beer, gone flat if possible (pour beer in a bowl and let it set for a few hours to let it go flat)

In a bowl, mix the dry ingredients well, then add the beer and stir until everything is mixed. Will keep up to 2 weeks refrigerated.

Mustard, Hot & Sweetly Dilled

Like all of these mustard recipes, you can package the dry mustard (called mustard flour) in a zip plastic bag with the recipe and a nice header tag to sell to your customers or give as gifts. This mustard is perfect for the buffet table next to sliced turkey and ham.

1 1/2 cups dry mustard
3/4 cup firmly packed brown sugar
3/4 cups cider vinegar
1 teaspoon salt
1/2 cup cooking oil
1 tablespoon dry or 2 tablespoons fresh dill weed

Place all of the ingredients, except the oil, in the food processor and turn on the lowest speed. While the food processor is running, slowly pour the oil through the top and blend until smooth. This is best aged in the refrigerator for at least a week before serving and will keep for up to 6 weeks refrigerated.

Omlet Seasoning, *dry*

1 tablespoon each: chives, chervil, basil and marjoram

Crush or grind coarsely. Use 1-2 teaspoons for a 3 egg omelet. Also good in egg salads, scrambled eggs and soufflés.

Omelet Seasoning, *fresh*

1 tablespoon fresh, chopped: parsley
2 teaspoons fresh, chopped chives
1 teaspoon fresh, chopped basil

Add to the eggs as they cook. Add a bit of chopped sweet or hot pepper and some cheese for a delightful omelet.

Pesto, *Traditional*

Pesto is a fresh, green herb blend made from herbs, cheese, nuts and oil. Called pistou in France and pesto or pistoli in Italy, this standard mix is served over hot pasta, pasta salad, on baked potatoes, even spread on bread for hors d'oeuvres.

1 1/2 cup fresh basil leaves, chopped
2 cloves garlic, diced or pressed
1/2 cup pine nuts, chopped (raw sunflower seeds work as a substitute)
3/4 cup grated Parmesan cheese
3/4 cup olive oil

Combine all ingredients, adding the oil last, Mix well. Will store in refrigerator overnight.

Pesto #2, *fresh*

2 cups basil
1 cup parsley
2 tablespoons sweet marjoram
1/2 cup pine nuts (or raw sunflower seed)
2 cloves garlic, minced
1/2 cup Parmesan or Romano cheese, grated
3/4 cup olive oil

Pesto #3, *Parsley Pistoli*

2 cups parsley
1/2 cup fresh spinach leaves
1/4 cup dill weed (the leaves, not the seed)
1/4 cup pine nuts or sunflower seed
1/2 cup Parmesan or Romano cheese, grated
3/4 cup olive oil

Chop fine in small food processor then add the oil. For variation, use thyme, summer savory or sweet marjoram in place of the dill weed.

Pickling Spice #1

2 tablespoon each:
whole allspice, whole coriander, broken cinnamon pieces and ginger root pieces
1 tablespoon each: whole cloves and mustard seed
1 teaspoon each:
crumbled chili pepper and cardamom seed
2 crushed bay leaves

Makes about 3/4 cup spice blend. Use in making fresh or canned pickles. Can also be used for shrimp or seafood boil blend.

Pickling Spice #2

2 tablespoons mustard seed
1 inch piece of dry ginger
2 tablespoons black peppercorns
2 teaspoons dill seed
2 teaspoons mace (whole, crumbled)
1 small dried hot pepper
4 cinnamon sticks, broken
2 teaspoons whole allspice
2 teaspoons whole cloves
2 teaspoons coriander seed
8 bay leaves, broken

Mix and store until ready to use. Sell by small packets with header tag and pickle recipe attached.

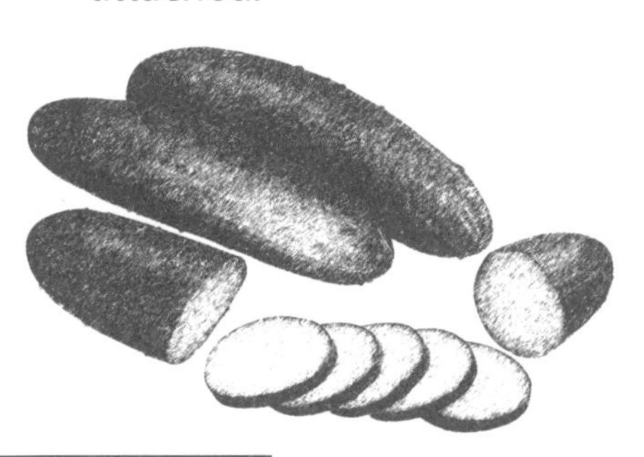

Pizza Seasoning

2 tablespoons each: onion flakes and dried sweet pepper flakes
1 tablespoon each: oregano, basil, parsley, thyme, marjoram and celery flakes
1/2 teaspoon each: crushed chili pepper flakes and crushed fennel seed

Sprinkle over tomato sauce on pizza. For even better flavor, combine 2 cups tomato sauce with 1 tablespoon Pizza seasoning. Simmer on low heat for 5 minutes before spreading over pizza dough.

Pizza Sauce, *fresh*

2 tablespoons oregano, stems removed
1 tablespoon basil
2 cloves garlic
1/2 teaspoon fennel seed (fresh or dry)
1 small onion, diced

Chop ingredients well by hand or in food processor. Combine with 12 ounces tomato sauce, a bit of water, 3 teaspoons sugar, simmer until reduced a bit, then spread on pizza dough.

Pizza Sauce, *fresh*

2 tablespoons oregano, stems removed
1 tablespoon basil
2 cloves garlic
1/2 teaspoon fennel seed (fresh or dry)
1 small onion, diced

Chop ingredients well by hand or in food processor. Combine with 12 ounces tomato sauce, a bit of water, 3 teaspoons sugar, simmer until reduced a bit, then spread on pizza dough.

Poultry Seasoning

2 tablespoons sage
1 tablespoon each: thyme and rosemary

Grind to a fine powder in a blender. Use 2 teaspoons per average-sized chicken (2 to 3 pounds), and for making stock, gravy base, etc. Also excellent seasoning for cornbread stuffing in turkey, duck, chicken or goose. (For goose stuffing increase the amount by 1/2 teaspoon and add 3 tablespoons parsley).

Poultry Seasoning #2

2 tablespoons each: summer savory, chives, rosemary, basil, chervil

Mix and pulverize or grind. Use 2 teaspoons per 2-3 pound chicken in cooking stock.

Poultry Seasoning #3, *European*

2 tablespoons each: tarragon, summer savory, thyme, parsley and dried orange peel

Grind to a fine powder. Use 2 teaspoons per chicken when making stock.

Poultry Seasoning #4

1 tablespoon each: sage, thyme, onion flakes, marjoram
1 teaspoon each: celery seed, cayenne and black pepper

Grind to a fine powder. Use about 1/2 tablespoon per chicken.

Poultry Seasoning #5

2 teaspoons each: sage, parsley, celery leaf and marjoram
1 teaspoon summer savory
1 teaspoon thyme

Pumpkin Pie Spice, *traditional*

1 tablespoon cinnamon
1 teaspoon ginger
1/2 teaspoon cloves
1/2 teaspoon nutmeg

Use this amount for one large can of pumpkin, which makes two pies when combined with eggs, sugar and condensed milk.

Pumpkin Pie Spice, *best*

This is a far superior pumpkin pie spice to other blends and came from our dear friend, Anne Kroboth.

Thank you, Anne!

8 tablespoons cinnamon
6 tablespoons nutmeg
3 tablespoons ginger
2 tablespoons cloves
2 tablespoons allspice

Package 5 1/4 teaspoons of the mix per zip bag and sell with a recipe attached. One packet is enough for 2 pies, using 1 large can of pumpkin, 6 eggs, 1 1/2 cups sugar, 1 can evaporated milk, 1 teaspoon vanilla and dash of salt. This is a classic pumpkin pie, better than the earlier pumpkin pie seasoning blend (and lots better than the recipe on the side of the pumpkin can!)

Quartre Epices or Spice Parisenne

1 tablespoon ground cinnamon
1 teaspoon each (ground):
cloves, ginger and nutmeg

Mix well. Use with yellow vegetables, beans, pea soup, broiled meats.

Salt Substitutes

No-Salt

1 tablespoon garlic powder
1/2 tablespoon basil
1/2 tablespoon oregano
1/2 tablespoon dehydrated lemon juice

Blend well in blender or food processor and use (or sell) with salt shaker.

Spicier No-Salt

3 tablespoons basil
2 tablespoons each: summer savory, celery seed, cumin, sage and marjoram
1 tablespoon lemon thyme.

Blend well in blender or food processor and use (or sell) with salt shaker.

No-Salt #3

1 tablespoon each: cloves, black pepper and coriander
2 tablespoon dried rosemary

Blend well in blender or food processor and use (or sell) with salt shaker.

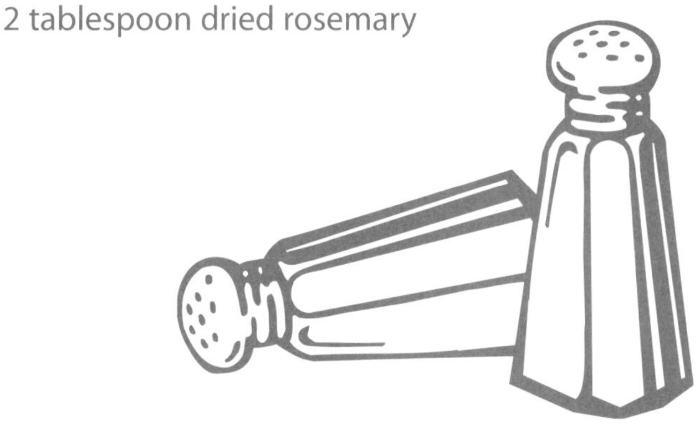

Sausage Seasonings

Sausage Blend, Cornell

1/2 teaspoon freshly ground black pepper
1/2 teaspoon crushed sage
1 teaspoon salt.

This is enough seasoning to mix with 1 pound ground pork. Lots of country sausage is made this way. The addition of crushed mild or hot peppers is also added to taste.

Sausage Seasoning, Polish

1 1/2 ounce black pepper
1 ounce ginger
1/2 ounce allspice
1/2 ounce salt
1 1/2 ounce nutmeg
1/2 ounce paprika
2 teaspoons garlic powder

This recipe makes enough seasoning for several pounds of meat. Often used with half smoked pork and half smoked venison for wild game sausage. The only other additional ingredients are 4 ounces water and 1/2 pound dry milk powder. Ingredients are mixed, then ground once again before being stuffed into sausage casings.

Sausage Seasoning, Spicy

2 tablespoons each: thyme, summer savory and marjoram
1 teaspoon ground bay
2 teaspoons black pepper
Optional: 1 tablespoons coriander seed, ground

This is enough seasoning to make about 8 pounds of spicy, but not hot, sausage. For hotter sausage, add crushed red peppers.

Sausage Seasoning #4

1/2 teaspoons each: sage, marjoram and thyme
1/8 teaspoon summer savory
1/2 teaspoon black pepper
2 teaspoons salt

This is enough seasoning to make 2 pounds of sausage.

Seafood Seasonings

Seafood Blend #1

2 tablespoons each:
marjoram, summer savory, thyme
1 tablespoons each: chervil and parsley
2 teaspoons fennel seed, crushed

Seafood Blend #2

2 tablespoons each:
mustard seed, dill seed, ginger, crushed chili pepper
2 bay leaves, crushed
1 tablespoons each:
whole allspice, celery seed, crushed cinnamon and black pepper corns

Use 1 tablespoons per 3 quarts of water.

Seafood Seasoning, powdered

1 tablespoons each:
dill weed (not seed), parsley, lemon basil
2 teaspoons each:
tarragon and celery leaf

Grind to a fine powder. Use 1-2 teaspoons per average seafood casserole or sauce. Good used in shrimp salad or any seafood and egg dish combinations.

Suggestion:

Feature a different seasoning in your shop or booth on a regular basis. Offer a free recipe which uses the seasoning, and have little samples for customers to taste. Taste samples are one of the best ways to sell seasonings and customers really appreciate the recipes and ideas.

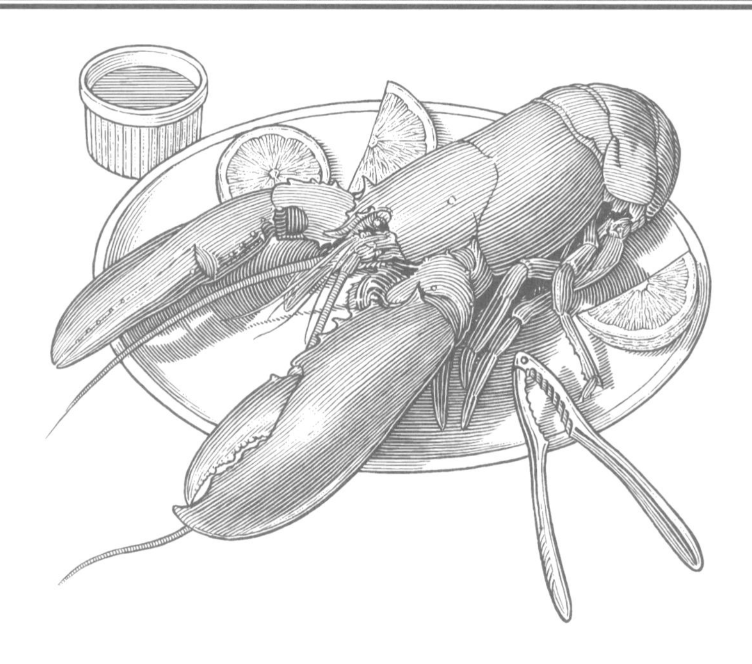

Miscellaneous

Soup Seasoning

Equal parts parsley, oregano, savory and thyme

Mix and crush well, adding to soup in the last 10 minutes of cooking.

Sweet Spice Blend

For yogurt, cereals, ice cream, flavoring for cakes and cookies.

2 tablespoons cinnamon
1 tablespoon each: ground orange peel, nutmeg, cloves and ginger

Try rolling plain sugar cookie dough in quarter sized balls, rolling each in this Sweet Spice Blend, then baking!

Thai Seasoning

2 tablespoons dehydrated tomato powder
1 tablespoons each: garlic powder, onion powder and paprika
2 teaspoons each: black pepper, cayenne, ground lemon peel and basil
1 teaspoon each: ground coriander, cilantro, white pepper

Mix and grind well to a fine powder. Use for Thai dishes, fried rice, stir-fry dishes, chicken, shrimp, etc.

Oregano
Chives
Sage
Personal
Body
Care
Bay
Dill
Basil
Tarragon

Bath Blends

Bath blends are a wonderfully relaxing method of soaking away aches and pains and of relaxing. The herbs work to soothe the body and the natural fragrances of the herbs and flowers, relax the mind.

General directions for all bath blends (and to include in the package so the customer knows how to use the product):

Use about 3/4 cup of bath herbs in a muslin drawstring bag. Pour very hot or boiling water over the bag of herbs in a pan and let the herbs steep like tea, while the bath tub is filling. Pour the hot bath "tea"' and the bag, into the tub.

After your bath the bag can be wrung out and hung on the tub's faucet to dry, then used one additional time. Bath herb bags can also be used by microwaving the damp bag and applying to specific sore places on the body, such as wrists, shoulder, etc.

The amounts listed are for large batches of bath blend. Mix the ingredients well and store in plastic bag inside a well sealed container. There are numerous ways to package these. You could put them in a half pound, attractive cellophane bag and attach three or four (rolled and tied with ribbon) 4 x 6 inch muslin drawstring bags. Or they can be packaged with one muslin drawstring bag attached to a 4 x 6 inch zip plastic bag (people seem to like to see the herb mix, thus the clear zip plastic bag method). I've also seen these packaged already in the cotton muslin drawstring bags, tied closed with 4 or 5 bags together in an outer plastic package. Whatever method you choose, be sure to package the finished product in a well-sealed plastic bag to keep insects out. Left in open air, the blend or the finished product is attractive to grain moths. Protect your products and keep them sealed away from these intruders!

Victorian Rose Bath Blend

This blend is wonderfully rosy and pleasant.

1 cup calendula
2 cups lavender
2 cups mint
7 cups roses
1/2 cup rosemary
several drops rose oil

Mix well and store in airtight container.

Relaxing Bath Blend

3 cups rosemary
3 cups shavegrass
5 cups roses
2 cups thyme
1 cup lavender
1 cup spearmint
2 cups calendula
4 cups epsom Salts
Optional:
few drops rose oil

Romantic Bath Blend

6 cups rosemary
1 cup catnip
1 cup shavegrass
1 cup calendula
6 cups roses
3 cups basil
3 cups thyme
4 cups epsom salts
*3 cups *borax*

**Twenty Mule Team Borax can be found in the laundry section of the grocery store. You can leave it out if you can't find any, but it's a wonderful water softener and is a mineral that makes the bath more pleasant. espom salts is available in the pharmacy.*

Sore Muscle Bath

3 cups spearmint
3 cups shavegrass
1 cup calendula
7 cups rosemary
2 cups marjoram
2 cups chamomile
1 cup catnip
2 cups thyme
1 cup lavender
1 four pound box epsom salts

Mix well and store in air-tight container. To use, put 1-2 cups in a cotton muslin drawstring bag, tie closed and pour 3 cups of boiling water over the bag and let it soak while the tub is filling. Then pour the bag and the "tea" into the bath tub and soak your sore muscles.

An alternate method for soaking carpal tunnel wrists or other specific spot, is to soak the bag and take it to work in a plastic bag. Then when breaktime comes, microwave the damp bag until very warm and apply it to the affected area several times throughout the day. Used this way, the herbs help the muscles relax and heal.

Magic Waters Beauty Bath

Ninan de L'Enclos, a French woman of the 18th century who was widely known for her radiant beauty, kept her breath-takingly good looks well into her 70s and attributed her youthful appearance to her daily magic waters beauty bath. Package the herbs and instructions in an attractive package and sell it next to your other bath products.

1/2 cup lavender flowers
1/2 cup chopped comfrey, root or leaves
1/2 cup thyme
1/2 cup rosemary
1 cup rose petals

Pour a quart of boiling water over the herbs and steep for 20 minutes. Strain. Pour liquid into the bath or sponge on.

Lavender helps reduce puffiness, comfrey is emollient and rejuvenating, especially to aging skin. Thyme is a mild deodorant as well as being antiseptic. Rosemary is energizing and astringent. Rose petals add relaxing, pleasant fragrance.

Bath Oils

We sold this as a kit, which included a packet of roses with the recipe and directions for the customer to make their own bath oil You might want to make up the oils yourself and sell them in attractive bottles. Displayed next to soaps and other body care products, they make an attractive impulse product.

Rose Bath Oil

1/2 cup rose petals
1 oz. light mineral oil
2 oz. glycerin (vegetable glycerin from the pharmacy)
4 drops red coloring for oils, optional
12 drops rose oil

Mix together, shake well and put 1-2 teaspoons in bath water.

Note: Regular food color is water or alcohol based and will not dissolve in oil. You will need to get an oil based food color from a kitchen specialty shop. It's not hard to find and does a great job of coloring oil based products.

Calendula Oil

Calendula has proven benefits for skin ailments. You can find calendulated oil or gel in the pharmacy, and it's recommended for soothing dry patchy skin, mild eczema, simple dry rashes, etc. Calendula oil is easy to use and can be kept for months and used when needed. Start with dried calendula flowers, either those you have grown, or good quality calendula from a reliable source.

Enough calendula flowers to fill a pint or quart jar
Vegetable oil (corn/canola blend is good)

Put the dried calendula flowers in the jar and pour enough vegetable oil to completely cover. Put a lid on the jar and let set for 10 days. Approximately every day, shake the jar to make sure the flowers and petals don't all settle to the bottom. You'll notice after the first day or so that the oil is taking on the dark yellow color of the flowers. That means the essential oils are being extracted correctly. At the end of 10 days, strain out the flowers and discard, saving the oil. (I often leave the flowers in, you can do it either way).
To use: dip your finger into the oil and massage in the effected area.

Massage Oils

These are used for sore muscles or simply for an oil to have applied while getting a body massage. Eureka Springs has been known for its mineral springs since before there were white settlers in northern Arkansas. For decades people came to drink the mineral waters and receive health giving massages. There are many massage therapists in town and one remaining historic bath house. Our friend and pharmacist, Jerry Stamps, concocted specific oils for regular customers for many years and the following formula is his own favorite.

Massage Oil, Jerry's

2 oz. almond oil
2 oz. sesame oil
10 drops lavender oil
10 drops rosemary oil
20 drops orange oil
20 drops lime oil

Mix and bottle until ready to use. Apply liberally over skin during massage. The fragrance is terrific and the oils are delightfully soothing and moisturizing for the skin.

Massage Oil, David's

David was an assistant in the Jerry's apothecary and this is one of his own concoctions. This is a delightful massage oil!

2 oz. almond oil
2 oz. apricot oil
5 drops sandalwood oil
5 drops snow pea oil
5 drops balsam oil
10 drops rose oil
5 drops cinnamon
3 drops vetiver oil
3 drops rosemary oil
2 drops lime
5 drops sequoia oil if available, if not use cedar oil

Mix well and bottle. Shake before each use.

Hair Rinses

Hair rinse products are best sold as a kit, with a packet of enough herbs to make a batch of rinse, with instructions for the customer. Packaged in a 4 x 6 inch zip bag with a recipe (and a 3 x 5 inch zip plastic bag of the herbs inside) along with a header tag, this sells well for those wanting to make their own herbal products.

Chamomile Hair Rinse

Chamomile hair rinse is especially good for light or blond hair, but is also pleasant for other colors, as well. Chamomile doesn't generally interact with hair colors, but if your hair is bleached or colored, you might want to try a section before using it on your entire hair.

Herbal hair rinses are mild and generally do not react with chemical dyes. If you use chamomile hair rinse on a regular basis, and are out in the sun a lot, you will notice a gradual lightening of the tips of your hair.

1 cup chamomile
4 cups water

Bring 4 cups of water to boil, and add 1 cup of chamomile flowers. Remove the pan from heat, cover with a lid and set aside until cooled to room temperature, or overnight. Strain the liquid, discarding the herbs. The rinse is now ready to use.

After shampooing your hair and rinsing with plain water, pour the chamomile rinse through your hair (you may choose to catch the chamomile rinse and use it a second time). Leave the rinse in the hair and dry as normal.

Note: left-over rinse should be kept in the refrigerator. You can add 2 teaspoons fresh lemon juice or 2 teaspoons of white vinegar to the liquid to help preserve it if keeping it longer than 3 or 4 days in the refrigerator.

We packaged these in 1 oz. zip bags with header tags. One ounce is enough for a batch of rinse, using 4 cups water, and the header tag should include the directions for making and using the rinse, or else tuck the instructions inside the packet on a 3 x 5 inch card.

Use these instructions for including with the package (for any of the hair rinses), if you are making this to sell:

Directions: Bring 4 cups of water to boil and immediately remove from heat, add the contents of the package (1 oz.) of the enclosed herbs, stir and cover with a lid. Let set until cool, or even overnight. Strain, discarding the flowers. The rinse is now ready to use.

After shampooing your hair and rinsing, pour the herbal rinse through your hair. You may choose to catch the rinse and re-use it one more time. Leave the rinse in the hair and dry hair as normal.

Rosemary Hair Rinse

This one is better for darker hair

1 cup rosemary
4 cups water

Sage Hair Rinse

This rinse is especially good for dark colored hair. While it won't significantly darken hair (and won't change gray) if used consistently it helps natural dark hair hold its color. More important, this is a pleasant hair rinse that removes soap residue and leaves the hair smelling pleasantly herby.

2 cups sage leaves (whole or broken)
4 cups water

Bring water to a boil, add the sage leaves, stir briefly and remove pan from heat. Cover with lid and let set overnight. Strain, discarding the herb and pour over freshly washed hair. You can heat the rinse slighly in the microwave before using and can catch and re-use the sage rinse for a second time.

Wild Hair Rinse

Hair a bit wild and unmanagable? Try this rinse.

1 cup rubbed Sage
4 cups nettles
2 cups shavegrass

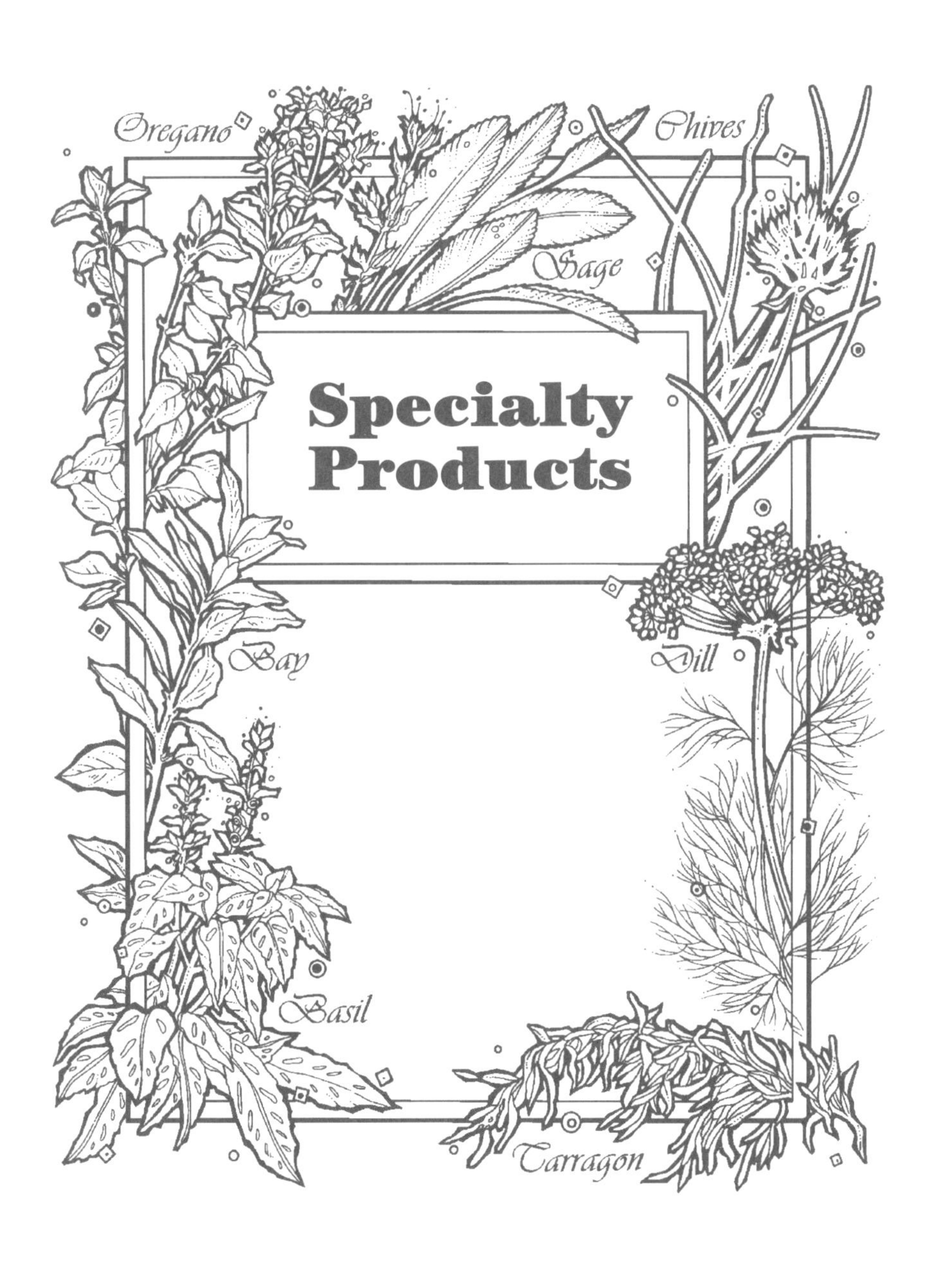
Oregano
Chives
Sage
Specialty
Products
Bay
Dill
Basil
Tarragon

Moth Repelling Blend

For use in closets, drawers or anywhere that you want to repel clothes moths.

(All ingredients dry)

4 cups fine cedar shavings (like those found in crafts shops where wood crafts are made, or buy them in pet stores where cedar shavings are sold in bundles for use as pet bedding)
2 cups tansy leaves
1 cup bay leaves
1 cup marigold blossoms (French marigolds, not calendula)
1/2 cup allspice berries
1/2 cup juniper berries
1 cup santolina (optional)

Mix well and sell in clear plastic bags, about a half pound each. Tie with ribbon and attach six 3 x 5 inch cotton muslin drawstring bags. The customer fills the little bags and ties them closed, then places them in drawers or ties them in the closet to repel insects. The bagged moth repelling blend, with cotton drawstring bags attached should sell for $6.95 to $9.95 per bag, depending upon your ingredients cost plus labor..

Hot Tub Blend

This blend of herbs is very pleasant for getting rid of the chlorine smell of the hot tub. We sold it for years in a 1/2 pound bag, with three 4 x 6 cotton muslin drawstring bags attached. To use, you simply put about a cup of the blend into the muslin bag, tie it closed securely so you don't get leaves in the hot tub, and throw it in. You can leave the herb bag in the tub for a couple of days then discard, or wring it out and use one additional time.

1 lb. eucalyptus leaves, whole and cut in half with scissors, or leaves already cut up
1 lb. shavegrass
1 lb. roses
1 lb whole mint leaves, or cut and sifted if whole ones are not available
1/2 lb. lemon balm
1/2 lb. lavender

Mix well and store in air-tight container out of sunlight or florescent light (both destroy the color, then the fragrance).

Hot Tub Blend, #2

3 lb. eucalyptus leaves
2 lb. lavender
2 lb. whole mint leaves
3 lb. roses

Mix well and store in air-tight container out of sunlight or florescent light Sell in the same way as the first Hot Tub Blend.

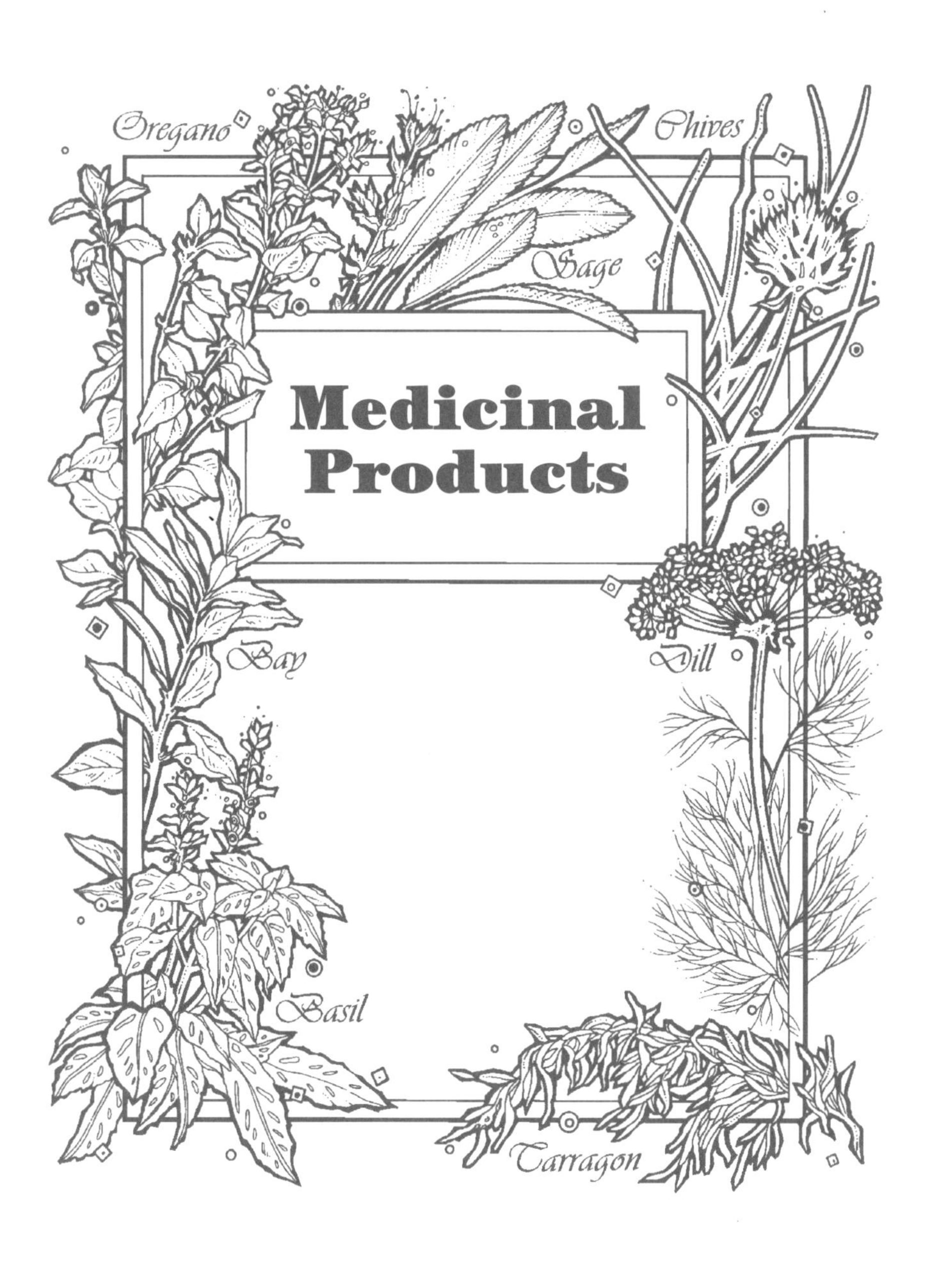
Oregano
Chives
Sage
Medicinal Products
Bay
Dill
Basil
Tarragon

Salves

You can put these products together like the teas and seasonings. Package enough of the herb and a tablespoon of beeswax, along with the recipe, in a zipper plastic bag to make one batch. Add a header tag and staple closed and your product is ready for sale.

Arnica Salve

Arnica is an herb known for its healing properties, especially on bruises. It's not recommended for use on open wounds or cuts.

1/4 cup petroleum jelly (such as Vaseline or you can use commercial Aquaphor Salve base from a pharmacy)
1 tablespoon dry arnica, chopped
2 tablespoons beeswax, shavings or small pieces

1. Place the petroleum jelly in a small, microwavable container and heat on the lowest setting. Heat in short sessions, 10 to 20 seconds at a time until the jelly is melted.
2. Add the arnica and mix well, then set aside overnight, covered with plastic wrap.
3. Heat the petroleum jelly again the same way as before, in 10 or 20 seconds at a time. When melted, strain out the majority of the arnica and discard.
4. Cut up the beeswax into small pieces and add to the petroleum jelly. Melt all in the microwave again in short sessions. When melted, mix well and let the spoon you've stirred with, cool in the air, about 1 minute. If the salve seems too runny, heat the liquid again with a bit more beeswax. Stir briefly and pour into a small container and cover.
5. To use, gently massage the salve into painful bruises.

Healing Comfrey Salve

This is an old-time salve useful for stings, bruises and simple injuries. Rather than make the salve itself, we made "kits" with all the ingredients, instructions and directions, and sold them that way. The customer then learned to make the product and could make their own in the future. We had an entire line of "Make Your Own" products that taught a process as well as gave the customer a good product.

(You will need)

1/2 cup dried, cut and sifted comfrey leaf

1/4 cup salve base (such as petroleum jelly or plain Vaseline) lard or commercial Aquaphor Salve base which can be ordered through many pharmacies

1 tablespoon beeswax, cut in small pieces

Double boiler or suitable pan for melting salve based and mixing salve (you can use a microwave on low setting if you do it carefully)

Kitchen spoon for stirring

Storage jar for finished salve

Begin by pulverizing the dried comfrey in a blender or food processor. Sift out any large pieces that don't break up, and discard.

Heat 1/4 cup salve base in a pan, preferably in double boiler, over water, until melted. Add the comfrey and mix, keeping the salve base hot, over the boiling water. Add the beeswax and mix until all the wax is completely melted and blended. Pour hot salve into small storage jar and cover with lid. Store the salve out of direct light, such as in the medicine cabinet.

To use, dip out a bit and rub on bruises, scratches and for other garden first aid.

Comfrey Salve, *fresh*

12 medium-sized tender comfrey leaves, fresh
1 bottle (about 16 oz.) aloe vera jel
2 teaspoons Vitamin E oil
1/4 cup rubbing alcohol

Put all of the ingredients in a blender and pulse-blend until the leaves are completely pulverized. Continue blending until the material is a smooth, green salve. Refrigerate in airtight container. This will last for several weeks. Use topically on cuts, scratches and other injuries to speed healing.

Light Calendula Salve

2 cups dried calendula flowers
1 tablespoon bees wax
olive oil

1 - Put the blossoms in a crock pot and pour enough olive oil to cover the flowers by about 2 inches. Turn the crock pot on lowest setting and leave overnight to slowly simmer. Pour out the contents and strain, letting the flowers drain to get all of the oil out, then discard the flowers.

2 - Warm the oil again in the crock pot and to each cup of oil, add 1 tablespoon of bees wax (you might want to shave or break the wax so it will melt faster). Mix well and pour into small plastic storage containers.

To use: Rub salve on affected areas.

Chickweed Salve

Chickweed is a healing plant, full of vitamins and chlorophyl. Chickweed salve is especially good for scratches, small bites and other first aid needs in the garden. You can even use this as a lip balm.

(You will need)
1/2 cup dried and chopped chickweed -
(make sure it is totally dry)
1/4 cup salve base (same kind used in Comfrey Salve, previous page)
2 tablespoons beeswax.

Pulverize the chickweed in a blender.
Heat 1/4 cup salve base in a double boiler, over water. Add the chickweed and stir well. Cover the pan and set it aside for a day.
Heat the chickweed/salve again over boiling water, stirring well. Continue stirring while adding the 2 tablespoons beeswax. Stir until the beeswax is completely melted and mixed in. Cover the pan and set it aside once more, for about a day. When totally cooled, check the salve to see if it is too thin or too thick. You want the salve to be thick enough as to not run, but not so thick that you can't dip a finger into it. If it is too thin, put the pan over boiling water again and add another tablespoon of beeswax. Or, if the salve is too thick, add a bit more salve base. Mix well and while melted, pour into salve jars for storage.

Horehound Cough Drops

This is the recipe for old-fashioned horehound cough drops. We sold 1/2 cup of horehound leaves with the recipe in a kit form. Here's the recipe:

8 cups boiling water
1/2 cup horehound leaves
4 cups sugar
1 1/4 cups dark cane syrup
1 tablespoon butter
1 teaspoon cream of tartar

Bring water to a boil and remove pan from heat. Add the horehound herb and set aside to let steep for 20 minutes. Strain, discarding the herb.

To 8 cups of this liquid, add 4 cups sugar, 1 1/4 cup syrup, 1 tablespoon butter and 1 teaspoon cream of tartar. Cook these ingredients until the liquid reaches the hard-crack stage (300 degrees on a candy thermometer).

Immediately pour into a well-buttered cookie pan, or any shallow pan with low sides, 10 x 15 inches or larger).

As the candy begins to cool, quickly score into pieces by running a buttered knife through the warm candy. Depending on the temperature of the room, the candy will set up faster or slower but should be hard enough to break in 5 minutes or less. After breaking the candy on the score lines, put candy, still warm, into a plastic bag with 1 cup of sugar and shake to coat candy. This keeps the candy from sticking together and should be stored in an air-tight bag or container. Use like candy or for coughing.

No-Itch Lotion

This is great for drying up poison ivy and for easing the sting and itch of chigger, tick and mosquito bites. Apply liberally everytime the itching starts. This works great!

Double handful young comfrey leaves and tender stems
Equal amount of heal-all (Prunella vulgaris)
Half as much plantain (Plantago major and/or P. lanceolata) as comfrey
12 spikes, or 1/2 cup, lavender flowers and stems
Same amount dock leaves (Rumex crispus) as plantain
1 1/2 gallons boiling water.

Add everything to the boiling water except the lavender. Push the herbs down with a spoon and make sure all the leaves are completely submerged and wilted. Let come to a near boil, remove from heat, add the lavender flowers and cover pan with a lid. Let steep overnight. The following day, discard the herbs and strain liquid well. To that liquid add:

1/2 cup goldenseal powder
1 quart bottle of cheap vodka
(this keeps the liquid from fermenting)

Let set 5 days. If the liquid appears to be fermenting (there will be a slight fizz and little bubbles around the edge) add another quart of cheap vodka. Generally you won't need to add the second vodka. Bottle in squeeze bottles and it's ready to use. This will keep for a year or more.

Century Tea

(also known as Essiac Formula)

This recipe supposedly was "discovered" by a nurse in Canada in the 1920s from an Indian healer there. It is a traditional cancer treatment among some northern Indian tribes and many people feel that it is still useful. Nurse Caisse (essiac is her name spelled backwards) believed the formula was useful for a variety illnesses where blood purifying and cleansing was useful. Her formula has been distributed widely and was given to me by a friend who had found the formula in Canada on a trip and had used it successfully.

1 oz. slippery elm bark (Ulmus rubra)
1/4 oz. rhubarb root (Rheum palmatum) Note: this is not garden rhubarb but a different variety, used for medicine.
4 oz. sheep sorrel (Rumex acetosella)
6 oz. powdered burdock root (Arctium lappa)

Instructions for use: Mix the dry ingredients. Bring 2 gallons of distilled or bottled water (not tap water, which may have chemicals added), to a boil in a stainless or enamel stockpot.

Add the dry ingredients and bring to a hard boil, then lower heat and let simmer for 10 minutes. Turn off the heat, cover the pot with a lid and allow to sit for 6 hours. Remove lid and allow to sit for another 6 to 8 hours, or overnight.

The following day, strain the liquid, discarding the herbs. Strain a second time if needed.

Divide the mixture into quart or gallon containers that are safe to freeze, and not filling to the top to allow for expansion during freezing. Put one quart in the refrigerator and put the remaining liquid in the freezer.

Using essiac: Once a freezer container of the formula is opened, it must be kept in the refrigerator. Shake the liquid, or mix up in a blender before using.

Take on an empty stomach, 2 to 3 hours after a meal. Combine 2 tablespoons essiac mixture in 1/4 cup hot spring or bottled water (you may want to whir this up in a blender as the slippery elm causes the mixture to be a bit gooey. Blending briefly simply makes it easier to swallow). Don't eat or drink anything for at least one hour after taking essiac mixture. Bedtime is a good time to take the mixture.

Allergy Eye Pillow

Rose Marie McGee, a long time plant friend and owner of Nichols Herb Seed Company, passed this formula along to us and said it was very useful to her for easing allergy swollen eyes.

This is the pattern for the eye pillow. You will need two pieces just alike. Sew all together except for about 2 inches on one end. Turn the pillow right side out (so that the sewn seams are inside), then fill with the herb/flax seed mix, filling about three-fourths full. Sew the remaining part closed and it's ready to microwave and use.

Note: Pattern has been reduced 50% to fit within the size format of the book.

1/2 cup spearmint
1/2 cup peppermint
1/2 cup lavender
1 cup eucalyptus
1 cup flax Seed

Mix together and put in a cloth bag and sew or tie closed. Heat in microwave for 45 seconds or so and apply to neck or forehead for relaxing and soothing. Note: be sure to launder the cloth first before sewing or filling, because the dyes and sizing in the cloth, when heated, can make the allergy worse instead of better.

Headache Eye Pillow

1 cup flax seed
1/4 cup lavender
1/4 cup peppermint

Mix and fill a small cloth bag with the mix and sew closed. To use: microwave for 45 seconds then apply while still warm to the closed eyes or forehead. It's soothing and pleasant. These sell well and if you make them from attractive cloth, can sell for higher prices than if you make them from less attractive cloth.

Dream Blends

If you aren't familiar with dream pillows, look for informaiton about the history and usefulness of dream pillows and dream blends in both my books,** "Making Herbal Dream Pillows" (Storey Publising) **and** "Profits from Dream Pillows" (Long Creek Herbs). **Dream Pillows make great selling gifts and customers love the delightful dreams they have. One blend, the Restful Sleep blend, is especially useful for children or adults that have nightmares. I first learned of this formula from a pharmacist, many years ago. Smokers who are using "the Patch" report that when using the Restful Sleep blend, they don't have the horrible nightmares that The Patch gives them.** "Profits from Dream Pillows" **gives more recipes, patterns, packaging information and marketing tips.

Pleasant Dreams

This is what I call a "generic good dream" blend.

2 cups roses
1 cup mugwort
1 cup lavender
1 cup marjoram
1/4 cup spearmint

Mix together well and use 2 tablespoons per pillow or 3 x 5 inch muslin drawstring bag

European Sleep Pillow

This is an old formula, used for centuries in various European cultures. It's meant to simply help children to drift off to sleep. Use a 3 x 5 muslin drawstring bag and stuff it full of this blend, placing it inside the child's pillowcase. (It works for adults, too).

1 tablespoon dill seed
1 tablespoon hops
1 tablespoon lavender
1 tablespoon roses

And this, also from an old European formula, to keep children from having nightmares:

1 tablespoon thyme
1 tablespoon chamomile
1 tablespoon roses
2 teaspoons marjoram

Birthday Dream Blend

We make this to present to friends on their birthday. Sew it up in a little cloth pillow (about 5 x 5 inches) or place the herbs inside a cotton muslin drawstring bag, tie it securely closed and place it inside the pillow case.

1 tablespoon roses
1/2 tablespoon lavender
1 tablespoon catnip
1 tablespoon mugwort
1 teaspoon hops
1 teaspoon linden flowers (if available)
1/2 teaspoon marjoram
1/2 teaspoon lemon verbena

Mix together well and place about 2 tablespoons of this blend in a 3 x 5 inch muslin drawstring bag, tie closed and place inside the pillowcase.

Suggestion:

Tips on making dream pillows for gifts or for sale:

Never, ever ever put oils of any kind in a dream pillow! Why? Two reasons.

1 - Essential oils, meaning those that come directly from plants, are too concentrated to be predictable. It takes large amounts of any herb or flower to produce the concentrated essential oils. For example, we understand that it takes about 100 pounds of fresh lavender flowers to produce one dram of essential oil. So, even a drop or two in a blend, can overpower the other fragrances.

2 - Fragrance oils sometimes contain some essential oils, but primarily contain chemicals and petroleum by-products. Those, when exposed to oxygen, begin to break down, in both pleasant and unpleasant ways.

The use of oils in dream blends is the best way to make an unreliable product that may give your customers or friends nightmares, headaches and a sick feeling upon waking. To avoid that - simply never, ever use oils in dream blends!

Another tip:

Always wash any fabric you use for dream pillows. Why? Because the sizing and dyes in all fabrics can cause headaches and nightmares. Simply wash the fabric first, with non fragrance detergent and without fabric softener. Your dream pillows will give you much better, and predictable results that way.

Restful Sleep Dream Blend

This one works great for children or adults. There is no noticeable dreams with this, just peaceful sleep without nightmares. It's also reported very beneficial for Vietnam veterans who have problems with flashback nightmares.

1 tablespoon hops
2 teaspoons marjoram
1 tablespoon mugwort
1 tablespoon roses

Mix together and place inside a cotton muslin drawstring bag, tie securely closed and place inside the pillowcase.

Gardener's Delight Dream Blend

We use this one sometimes when we do workshops in botanic gardens or herb conferences. In most people it evokes enjoyable and pleasant dreaming.

1 tablespoon mugwort
1 tablespoon roses
2 teaspoons catnip
2 teaspoons lemon verbena
1/4 teaspoon mint

Products for Men

Fish Odor Remover, for hands

Of course women can use this product, but we first developed it for the fishermen who came with their wives to visit the herb farm.

2 tablespoons rosemary
2 tablespoons sage
2 tablespoons thyme
2 tablespoons lemon verbena
1 tablespoons mint (use spearmint or peppermint)
3 cups white vinegar

In a non-aluminum pan, bring the vinegar to a boil and add all of the herbs and stir briefly. Cover pan with a lid, remove from heat, and let set overnight. The following day, strain out the herbs and discard, saving the liquid.

After fishing and cleaning fish, wash hands as normal, then soak hands in the Fish Odor Remover for a minute or two and dry without washing off the soak.

Mosquito Repellant

This pleasant smelling, herbal blend helps keep mosquitoes away. Simply splash some on, or put it in a spray bottle and spray clothes, back of neck, arms, etc. Use fresh herbs for this.

1 cup clary sage leaves (or leaves and flowers)
1 cup spearmint
1/2 cup pennyroyal
1/2 cup garden sage
1/4 cup lavender flowers
8 cups cheap vodka

Put the vodka in a jar large enough to contain all of the ingredients. Add the herbs, put a lid on the container and shake. Keep in the pantry or away from sunlight and shake daily for a week. Leave it alone for 5 days, then strain out the herbs and discard, and to the vodka-herb blend, add 2 cups bottled water. Rub on or use a sprayer to apply the repellant.

After-Shave

We have sold the dry herb mixture in 4 x 6 inch zipper plastic bags with instructions and header tag for use in gift baskets.

1 cup calendula flowers
1 cup lavender
2 1/2 cups roses
1/2 cup mint (spearmint or peppermint)
1/2 cup marjoram
1/2 cup lemon balm
1/2 cup lemon verbena
1 1/2 cups rosemary
6-8 whole cloves
4 or 5 whole allspice berries

Place all in a glass container and cover with cheap vodka. Cover with lid and shake daily for 10 days. Strain and discard herbs, then mix 2 cups witch hazel liquid from the pharmacy. Shake and bottle. Can be tinted lightly with food color.

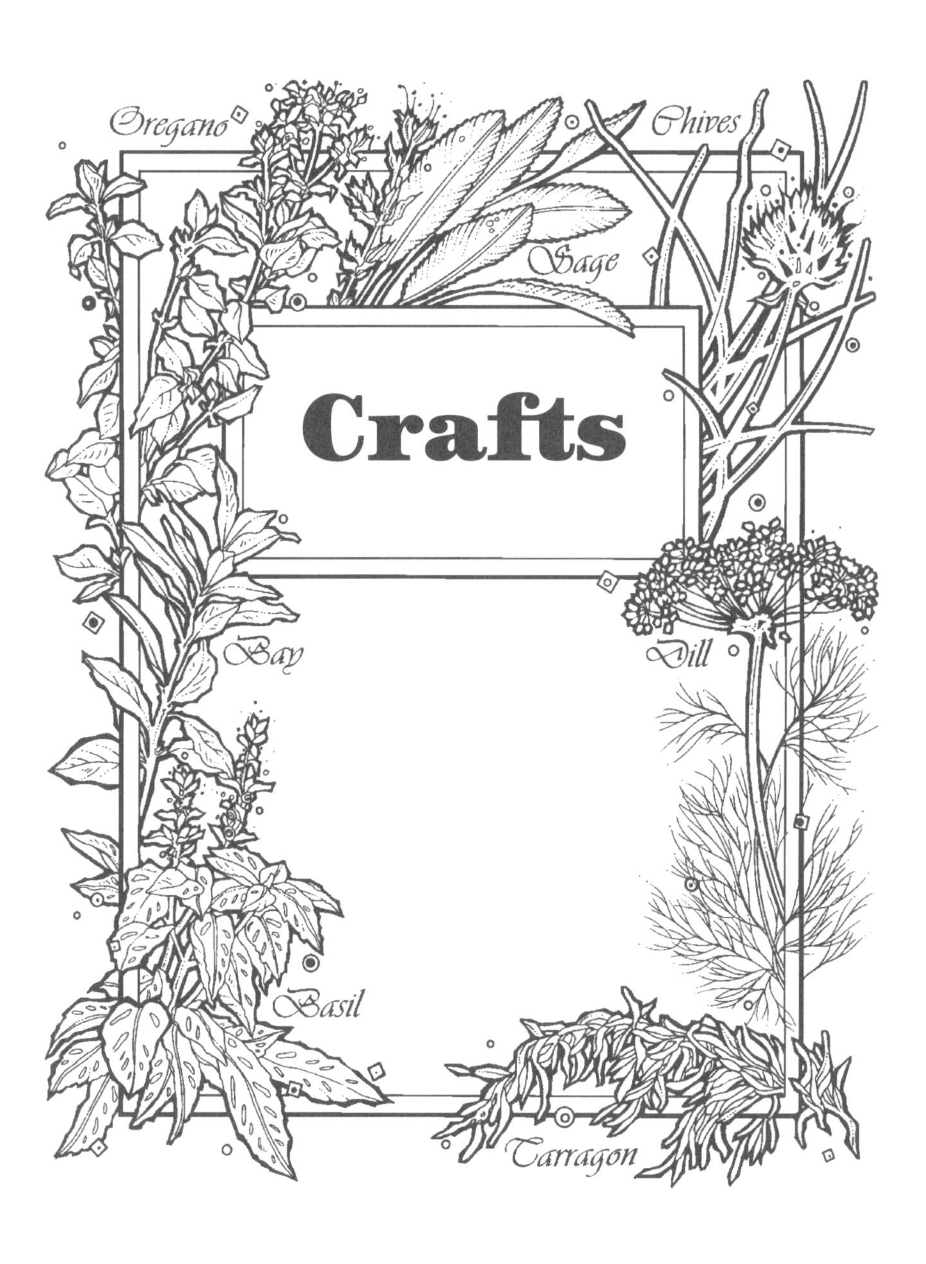
Crafts
Oregano
Chives
Sage
Bay
Dill
Basil
Tarragon

Catnip Mouse

This works well as a kit or as a finished product. There is more profit in selling the kit then there is in selling the finished catnip mouse, simply because of labor costs. The following page shows our instructions. The sheet is folded in half and placed inside a 4 x 6 inch zip plastic bag, alongside a piece of cloth cut to size, a piece of yarn for the tail and a 3 x 5 inch bag of our premium grade catnip. It's closed up with a header tag labeled "Make your own Catnip Mouse."

> **Note:**
>
> *The assembly instructions and header label for the Catnip Mouse kit have been included so that you can photocopy them to package with your own kits if you wish.*

Catnip Mouse Kit

Includes everything you need for making a Catnip Mouse for your cat:

- Pattern
- Cloth
- Yarn Tail
- Catnip
- Instructions

Note: This page is meant for photocopying and inserting inside your Catnip Mouse Kit.

Catnip Mouse Kit

The cloth for making your catnip mouse is enclosed and cut to size. Simply sew up the material, wrong-side out, leaving about 1 inch at the tail end, unsewn. Turn material right side out.

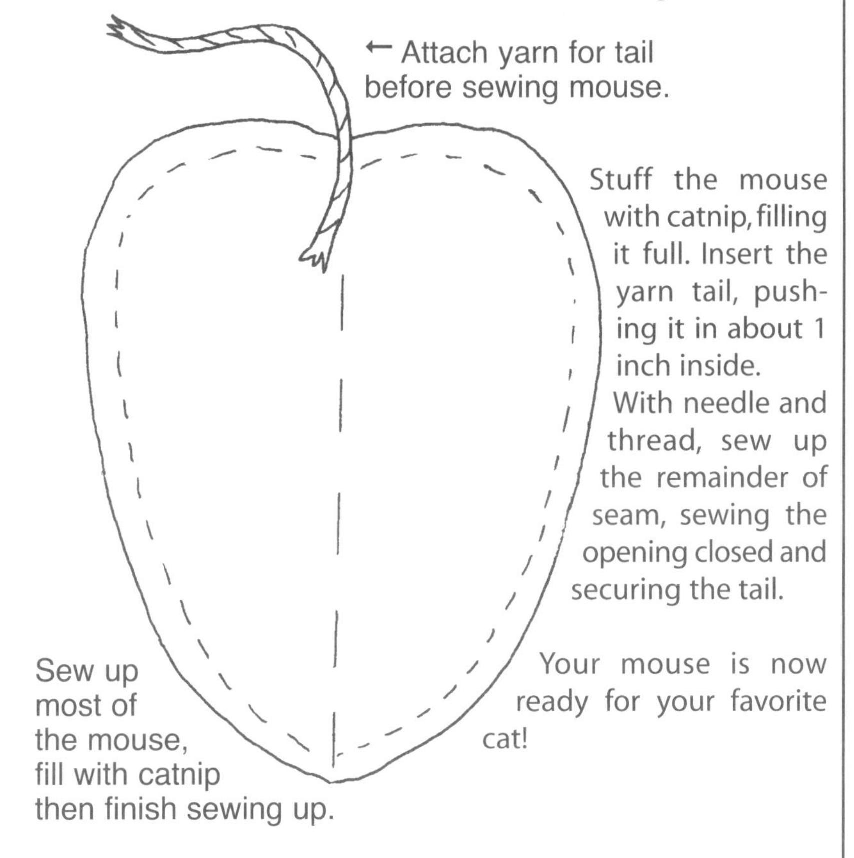

← Attach yarn for tail before sewing mouse.

Stuff the mouse with catnip, filling it full. Insert the yarn tail, pushing it in about 1 inch inside. With needle and thread, sew up the remainder of seam, sewing the opening closed and securing the tail.

Your mouse is now ready for your favorite cat!

Sew up most of the mouse, fill with catnip then finish sewing up.

Many people like to offer their cat the Catnip Mouse at different times of day, or only on special occasions. Cats seem to grow tired of their toy if it is available constantly, but get more enjoyment when the mouse is brought out on occasion for a special treat.

Your business name & address goes here......

Microwavable Relaxing Herbal Pillows

You've likely seen these being sold in malls where there are lots of people. The primary method for sales is to have a pillow already heated and when a customer walks by, offer to demonstrate the pillow by laying it around their neck, on their shoulders. They will immediately say, "Ooooh, aaaaahh!" The response is pleasant and immediate. Your sale is already made! Just remember to price these pillows at a price to sell. Normal price breaks (the number at which people most easily purchase something) are these: $9.95, $12.95 and $19.95. Don't be greedy and sell them too high. The profit in this product is great and it's better (we think) to sell a lot of products at a reasonable price than a few at a high price.

Microwavable Relaxing Herbal Pillow, #1

Here's the mixture to use in your Relaxing Herbal Pillow:

4 cups flax seed
1/2 cup lavender flowers

Mix well and place inside the cloth pillow and sew closed.

That's all! Some people making these add herbal oils to the pillow. Don't do it! There are a lot of folks who react negatively to herb oils, either through headaches or sneezing. Make a better product and leave out the oils! The lavender, which is a relaxing fragrance, will give off pleasant but mild fragrance, every time the pillow is microwaved for use.

You can also use rice, or rice and flax seed, or a mixture of flax and buckwheat hulls. Flax is inexpensive and holds heat a good length of time when microwaved. Don't use popcorn - it pops inside the pillow when it's microwaved.

Microwavable Relaxing Herbal Pillow, #2

4 cups flax seed
1/4 cup rose petals
1/4 cup lavender flowers

Cut out your cloth in the shape of a "U" (*see illustration on page 84*). Sew up the back side and sew seams inside for compartments (so that the seed and herbs don't all slide to one end or the other). Fill each compartment with the mixture and sew up the pillow. It's now ready for sale. We suggest you put a label on it with instructions. A little card, the size of a business card folded in half, is perfect. Run a string through it and pin to the pillow with a tiny gold safety pin. Include these instructions:

> Microwave the Relaxing Herbal Pillow on medium setting of the microwave for about 2 minutes, or until the pillow is pleasantly warm to the touch. Place the pillow around your neck, on your shoulders and feel your muscles begin to relax. May be used again and again.

This is half of the pattern for the shoulder microwavable pillow. The whole piece will be a "C" shape so that it will fit over the shoulder. The finished pillow should be about 14 inches long. Once you have layed out both halves of this pattern, you will need two pieces of cloth alike. Sew all sides, leaving about 2 inches not sewn, in order to fill the pillow with buckwheat or flax seed. Fill the pillow three-fourths full, then sew the remining piece closed.

Note:

Pattern has been reduced 50% to fit within the size format of the book.

Boot & Tennis Shoe Stuffers

This simple product will make your customers happy. The finished size is 1 3/4 inches across and about 6 inches long, sewn of attractive cloth. Put two in a zip plastic bag with instructions printed on the header tag.

These little stuffers remove moisture and odor from shoes. They work great and are easy to make and package.

Start with a 5 pound bag of cat litter, the lightweight, non-scented kind, or 5 pounds of vermiculite (found in the plant department of discount stores). Put that in a large container or plastic trash bag and add:

10 cups roses and petals
8 cups cedar shavings
2 cups lavender flowers
4 cups mint, any kind
2 pounds charcoal granules (found in the plant or aquarium department of many stores)
4 cups baking soda

In the plastic bag, which you have twisted closed, mix the materials well.

Sew up each pillow on 3 sides, fill with the mixture and sew the fourth side closed. Be sure to use tightly-woven cloth so that the baking soda doesn't filter through the cloth.

To use: Place one Boot and Tennis Shoe Stuffer in each shoe at night or when storing. Once a week, leave the Stuffer in the sunshine for a few hours to rejuvenate.

The finished tenny-stuffer should be about 2 inches across and about 5-6 inches long. Sew up all except one end, then stuff and finish sewing.

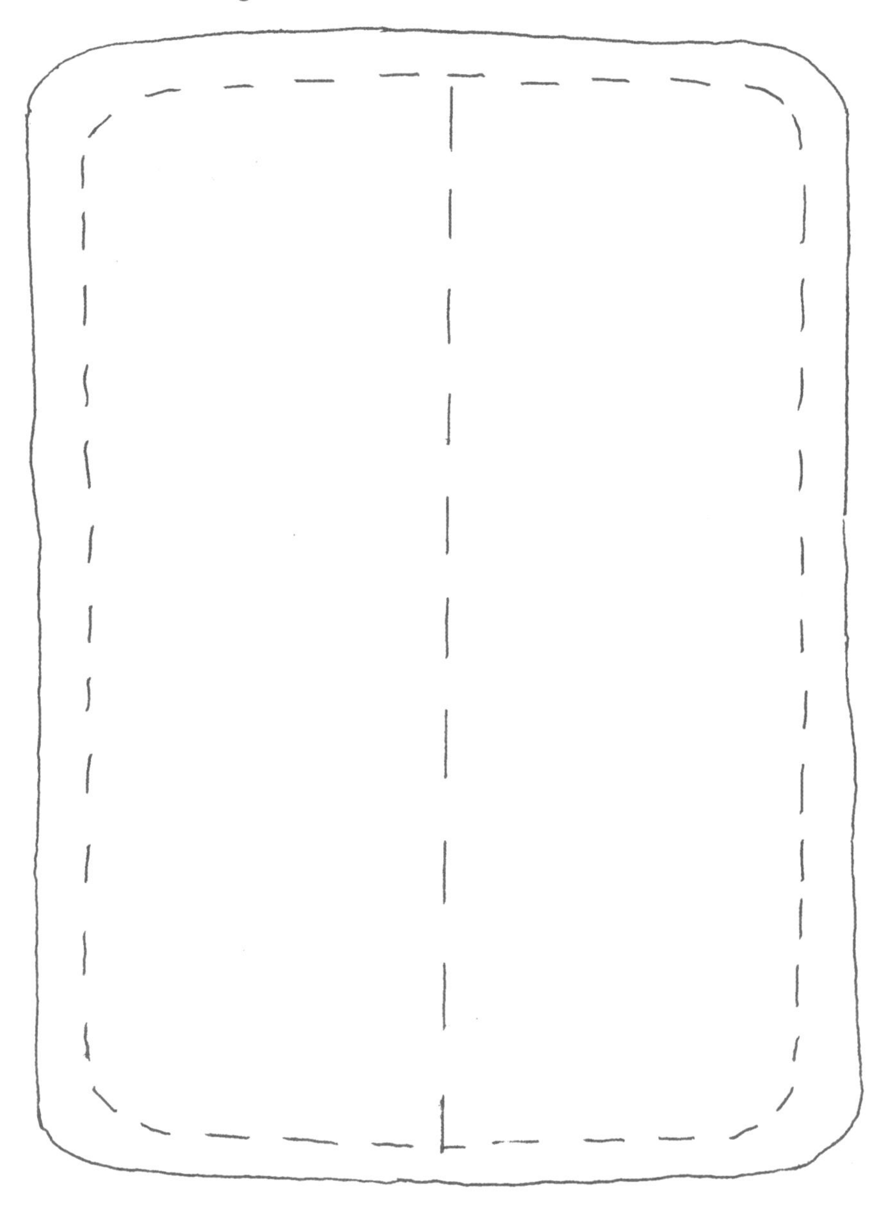

Oregano
Chives
Sage
Pet
Products
Bay
Dill
Basil
Tarragon

Doggie Treats

If you have customers who have pets, you might consider adding a line of pet products to your store. Ready made gourmet dog biscuits and cat treats are great sellers, especially around the holidays. Invite your customers to come in for a special "tasting" event, bringing their pets to sample your pet products. If the pet likes the treat (and it will) you've got certain sales.

Make these up like cookies, cutting them out with dogbone shaped cookie cutters (or birds for cats) and package them a dozen or two to a crystal clear ellophane bag (boutineer bags like the florist uses are perfect). Close with a ribbon and a stick-on label with the flavor noted.

Cheese Flavored Dog Cookie

2 cups whole wheat flour
1/2 cup cornmeal
1 1/2 tablespoons dried parsley
1/2 teaspoon dried or fresh chives, chopped
1/2 cup grated romano or parmesian cheese
1 egg
1/4 cup vegetable oil
1/2 cup water
1 clove garlic, minced fine
1 tablespoon bone meal, optional (the kind from the pet store, not the bone meal used in the garden)

Mix and roll out to about 1/2 inch. Cut with cookie cutter and bake at 350° for about 30 minutes or until golden brown. When finished baking, turn off the heat and leave the cookies in the oven for another 30 minutes to harden.

Vegetable Dog Cookie

Use left-over cooked vegetables for this:

2 cups whole wheat flour
1 cup finley chopped vegetables such a carrots, potatoes, corn, etc.
2 teaspoons any season-all product (Mrs. Dash, etc.)
1 tablespoon onion, chopped very fine
1 egg
1/4 cup vegetable oil
1 tablespoon bone meal, optional

Preheat oven to 350°. Mix the vegetables, egg, oil and onion, then add the remaining ingredients and mix again. Add enough water, or the water the vegetables were cooked in, to make a firm dough. Mix well then roll out like cookie dough, cutting out with cookie cutter and baking on an oiled cookie sheet for 30-40 minutes. Turn off oven heat at the end of cooking and let the cookies set for another 30 minutes to harden.

Healthy Dog Cookie

2 cups whole wheat flour (or use a mixture of flours, such as oat, 9 grain, rice four, etc.)
1/2 cup cornmeal
1 teaspoons any season-all product (Mrs. Dash, etc.)
1/2 teaspoon garlic powder
1 egg
1/4 cup vegetable oil
1/2 cup milk

Preheat oven to 350°. MIx flours, seasonings, then the egg, oil and liquid. Mix in a food processor or by hand. If batter is too stiff, add a bit of water. Roll out on a floured surface until 1/2 inch thick. Cut with cookie cutter and place cookies on a cookie sheet. Bake for 30 minutes or until golden brown. Turn off the oven and leave the cookies in the oven for another 30 minutes to harden.

Beefy Dog Cookies

2 cups whole wheat flour
1/2 cup cornmeal
2 tablespoons dried parsley
2 teaspoons chopped dried chives or onion flakes
1 egg
1/4 cup vegetable oil
1/2 cup beef broth (cooked or canned)
1 teaspoon Kitchen Bouquet

Preheat oven to 350°. Mix all ingredients well and roll out on floured surface, cut with cookie cutter and bake for 30 minutes. Turn off oven heat and leave cookies in for another 30 minutes to harden.

Doggy Breath Mint Cookie

Great for getting rid of doggy breath!

2 cups whole wheat flour
1/2 cup cornmeal
1/4 cup dried parsley
2 tablespoons dried spearmint
1 egg
1/4 cup vegetable oil
1/2 cup water or vegetable broth

Preheat oven to 350°. Mix ingredients well, roll out on floured surface, cut with cookie cutter and bake for 30 minutes. Turn off oven as in previous recipes.

Catnip Cat Cookie

2 cups whole wheat flour
1/2 cup cornmeal
1/4 cup dry, finely chopped catnip
1 egg, beaten
1/4 cup vegetable oil
1/2 cup vegetable or meat stock

Preheat oven to 350°. Mix all ingredients and roll out on a floured surface to 1/4 inch thick. Cut with tiny cookie cutter (bird or dog shaped works great) and place on oiled cookie sheet. Bake for 30 minutes or until golden brown. Turn off oven heat and leave inside the oven to firm up the cookies, for another 30 to 45 minutes. Let dry a day or two before packaging.

Note:

See section on Crafts, for instructions for making a Catnip Mouse.

How to Price Your Product

There are numerous methods for establishing a price for a product and several examples are given here. You can choose the method that most fits what you want for your business.

Method #1

Add up the cost of the ingredients and double it.

Let's say that you are making a spice blend. You figure out that your costs are as follows:

Ingredients	*0.65*
Package	*0.20*
Label	*0.10*
Labor	*0.15*
Total Cost	**1.10**
Retail price	2.20

Some businesses will simply double the cost to arrive at the retail price. Using this method, you would sell the product for $2.20. Method #1 may short change you on your labor.

What if you want to wholesale the product? How much discount do you give and how do you arrive at a fair price for your time, materials and labor?

An easy way to determine labor cost: *Time yourself, or an employee, for 15 minutes. Count the number of packages made during that time and take that number times 4, to get the hourly cost. Using the real cost per hour (hourly wage plus insurance, FICA and any other costs involved in that person working for you), divide the cost per hour by the number of the products made and you will have a per item cost.*

Method #2

Actual value method.

Notice that on method #1, there was no allowance for incidental costs. Nothing was included for insurance on the building, on electricity, heat, cooling, garbage pickup. Those should be figured in, as well.

Worse, you may have included nothing for labor cost if you were making the product yourself. "After all," you thought, "I wasn't doing anything anyway, so it didn't cost me anything for labor." You're making a big mistake if you put such a low value on your time. You're establishing the cost of a product, based on free labor. What happens when you are so successful that you have to hire help? Your prices will have to go up, of course!

Look at the **$1.10** cost of the product. Is it a fair cost assessment? A more realistic price structure would be this:

Ingredients	*0.65*
Package	*0.20*
Label	*0.10*
Labor	*0.15*
Incidentals	*0.60*
Total Cost	**1.70**
Wholesale	3.40
Retail price	5.50 - 6.95

This method is more realistic in covering your actual costs of putting the product together and allows you some profit for creating more products.

Method #3, the Multi-Level Formula

According to the Small Business Office at our local collge, the formula for deciding on the price for a product is to multiply the cost of the product times 5. (The cost of the product is the material, labor and packaging cost). If you start with a cost of $1, then you would have a retail cost of $5 for the product.

By this formula, you would charge a wholesale price of $2.25. The wholesaler would charge their retailer $2.75, and they in turn would charge the retail customer $5.

This method works pretty well if you are going to sell to a wholesaler or distributor, who sells to a retailer who then marks the product up. But this method leaves out one important aspect of selling herbal products - *the perceived value.*

Method #4, Perceived Value

I attended a workshop years ago given by "Herbal Ed," the founder of the HerbPharm company in Oregon. They make high quality herbal tinctures and have been in business for many years.

In the workshop, Ed held up one of his one ounce amber tincture bottles for the audience to see. He said, "I can make this product for about $1 a bottle. But I have learned that if I sell it for $2 a bottle, the normal mark-up of similar products, people won't buy it. Worse, I become disenchanted because there's no real incentive for me to create new products."

Ed went on to explain that with a product like an herbal tincture, he had learned that his customers just didn't take the product seriously if they paid $2 a bottle. Sure, it made him a profit - wouldn't anyone be happy to double their money every day?

The problem, he explained, was in the perceived value of the product. The customer looks upon the product as cheap. "I only

paid $2 for this bottle, it's probably not very good," and they'd put it aside on the shelf and not use it.

"And I want them to use my products," he said. "I make very good tinctures, they work, people get better or feel better after using my products. The hard part is getting them to take seriously my product in order to actually use it."

He went on to explain about the perceived value of any product. "The more you pay for a product," he said, "the more you see the product as useful."

Additionally, he told us that by only doubling his money, it didn't give him incentives to do what he does best, which is to research and develop newer and better products.

So what was his solution? He sold the product that cost him $1.00, for $9.95. Quite a markup, wouldn't you say? However, his customers no longer set the bottle on the shelf. They had shelled out good, hard-earned money and they darned sure were going to get their money's worth! They used the product and discovered that it was an outstanding product. Further, Herbal Ed had enough cash from the sales of his products to enlarge his research facility and to research and develop newer and better products.

Here's the formula for the retail price, based on the perceived value:

Ingredients	*0.65*
Package	*0.20*
Label	*0.10*
Labor	*0.15*
Incidentals	*0.60*
Perceived value	*4.00*
Retail price	**5.70**

Is it fair to mark the product up that much? Of course it is. If you don't, and you sell your product too cheap, you're not going to pay the bills. You'll get disillusioned and tired of making the product because there's so little incentive and profit.

Look at the product and try to see it the way your customer sees it. Is it a shabby product that only looks like a $2 product? If so, then the perceived value is at its limit. You can either improve the product, or continue to make a cheap, not very good product which you sell cheaply. More than likely, if you are doing that, customers won't buy the product and you'll wind up throwing it out. Worse, you won't stay in business very long.

Instead, look at the product. Make it look good. Put it in a good package, with a nice label. Make sure the product is good, something that you would be proud to use yourself. Price it high enough that the customer is proud, also, to take the product home. Price it so that the customer takes the product seriously, and will use it. Price it in such a way that you are pleased with the profit; not only do you cover your costs, but you have enough profit to encourage you to want to make more products.

Note:

Where you package your products is important:

If you plan to make seasonings and edible products you will need to check on your state's laws on packaging such products. The State Health Department is the office responsible for inspecting restaurants and packaging facilities. If you are a small business, you may not be able to afford the $10,000 to $25,000 investment in building your own state approved kitchen for making your products.

An option that you might want to explore is renting space in a state approved kitchen, such as a Senior Center or restaurant that is only open limited hours per day. Senior Centers generally only use their kitchen for a few hours in the morning and during the lunch hour. Those kitchens have to be state approved and inspected regularly. Visit with the manager of the Senior Center and see if he or she will rent you space in the kitchen to do your packaging for a small fee. Keep records of the time you spend and keep those on file, to prove your products have been packaged in a state approved kitchen.

Sources

Bags, for Packaging

Action Bag

501 N. Edgewood Ave.
Wood Dale, IL 60191
800-824-2247
www.actionbag.com

Action Bag is very nice to deal with. The offer zip plastic bags, boxes, tissue paper, cotton muslin drawstring bags and more.

Nashville Wraps

1229 Northgate Business Parkway
Madison, TN 37115
800-547-9727
www.nashvillewraps.com

Good selection of gift wraps, customer shopping bags and other things. Their web-site isn't easy to use (you need a password to shop!) and their minimum order is $50, so if you're out of something, they charge you a surcharge for smaller orders. But their selection is good.

Bags & Bows

33 Union Ave.
Sudbury, MA 01776
800-225-8155

Oils, Bottles, Glycerine, Jars

Lavenderlane.com

Offering decorative and packaging bottles and jars, in polished aluminum, glass and plastic, in any quantity. You can order one or a thousand from these folks. Their on-line site is simple and easy to use.

Containers, Bottles & Jars

International Plastics, Inc.

185 Commerce Center
Greenville, SC 29615
800-433-4043; 803-297-8000

Custom printed zip bags and other industrial packaging materials.

Mod-Pac Corp.

1801 Elmwood Ave.
Buffalo, NY 14207
800-666-3722; 716-873-0640

Mod-Pac offers a wide assortment of boxes for candies, cookies. They offer boxes with clear plastic fronts that are perfect for dream pillows and pet cookie products.

Richards Packaging, Inc.

9050 Cody
Overland Park, KS 66214
800-446-4080

SKS Bottle & Packaging So.

3 Knabner Rd.
Mechanicville, NY 12118
518-899-7488

Transparent Container Co.

345 N. Western Ave.
Chicago, IL 60612
312-666-4413

Offes clear plastic containers, perfect containers for doggie cookies.

US Can Co.

8901 Yellow Brick Rd.
Baltimore, MD 21237
410-686-6363
West Coast sales office: 209-835-6955

U.S. Can offers plain tin and decorative tin containers of all kinds. Perfect for cookies, foods, seasonings.

Bulk Herbs & Books (ours)

Long Creek Herbs

P.O. Box 127
Blue Eye, MO 65611
417-779-5450
Email: Lcherbs@tri-lakes.net
www.Longcreekherbs.com

Offering bulk herbs and books by Jim Long, both wholesale and retail. No minimum order. Ask for wholesale price list.

Bees Wax

Mid-Continent Agrimarketing, Inc.

8909 Lenexa Dr.
Overland Park, KS 66214
913-492-1640 • 800-547-1392

Bees wax for salves as well as other bee supplies.

Boxes

Mid-Atlantic Packaging

14 Starlifter Ave.
Dover, DE 19901
800-284-1332

Offering both ready made and custom made small boxes and containers for food and non-food products.

Cookie Cutters

NCreative House International Corp.
P.O. Box 127
East Greenville, PA 18041
215-541-4971

Offer dogbone, bird and other shaped cookie cutters.

Tissue Paper

Action Bag
501 N. edgewood Ave.
Wood Dale, IL 60191
800-824-2247
www.actionbag.com

Labels, Sticker, Tags

Action Bag
501 N. edgewood Ave.
Wood Dale, IL 60191
800-824-2247
www.actionbag.com

Mid-Atlantic Packaging
14 Starlifter Ave.
Dover, DE 19901
800-284-1332

Offering a large assortment of ribbons and labels. Notable are their natural kraft labels, useful for shops that want a natural looking label for their products.

Index

Index